CONQUER STICKY SITUATIONS

A Fresh and Empowering Approach to
Tough Talks at Work and in Life

JILL SHROYER

CONTENTS

Library of Congress Control Number: 2020924752

ISBN (ebook): 978-1-7362134-1-4

ISBN (print): 978-1-7362134-0-7

FREE AUDIOBOOK

Just to say thanks for buying my book, I would like to give you the Audiobook version 100% FREE!

To download, go to:

conquerstickysituations.com/audiobook

FREE WORKBOOK

Grab your FREE Conquer Sticky Situations Workbook!

conquerstickysituations.com/workbook

The workbook includes:

• Recap of 5-step formula

• Dedicated space to complete the *You Got This!* exercises and *Personal Development Challenges* from the book

• BONUS exercises to expand on what you learn

To my husband, Dan, and my munchkins, Ty and Jenna, for giving me
the greatest gift, the gift of time to be able to
get this book out into the world.

To Cyndi, who inspired me to write a book
and whose advice will always stay with me:
Keep on pedaling and don't freak out.

"Don't be afraid of new ideas. Be afraid of old ideas. They keep you where you are and stop you from growing and moving forward. Concentrate on where you want to go, not on what you fear."

—Tony Robbins

MY WRITING INSPIRATION

A deep blue sky stretched as far as you could see over the mountains of Park City. The air was crisp and cool with a hint of fall. The trail was free of its typical dust. It was damp and tacky from the quick rain earlier in the day. I followed Cyndi up Armstrong Trail.

One of my favorite things about summers in Park City is the Team Sugar Tuesday night women's guided mountain bike rides. Team Sugar is a women's riding group in Park City, which was co-founded by my friend Cyndi Schwandt in the late 1990s. I've been riding with the group ever since I came to Park City in 2001, nearly 20 years ago. Team Sugar referred to Cyndi as "the pioneer" of the Park City mountain biking community. She always found the most obscure and off-the-beaten-path trails and connectors, having built many of the trails herself years ago. If there was one person who embodied everything about living in our mountain town, it was Cyndi. She loved every mountain sport, from skiing to biking and hiking. An active Park City community member, Cyndi volunteered doing trail maintenance, frequented the local farmers market, and took part in ski conditioning classes at the local gym.

Cyndi's legs powered her up in front of me as if she were riding on a flat road, showing her ease and grace on a mountain bike. I let my mind wander as I reflected on the peacefulness of the early evening when I heard Cyndi call back to the group. "There's a technical section coming up. Keep on pedaling. Hey Jill! Don't freak out!" Cyndi knew me well enough to know I got anxious when approaching technical sections of the trail. I'd often panic and unclip from my pedals and hike over the technical rocky sections. Cruising uphill on a dirt single-track trail is where I'm happy as a New England clam at high tide. Self-talk is essential to get myself through the rocky parts, often out loud. "You can do this, Jill! Go! Go!" I did best in those sections when I focused on gazing past the rocks, breathing, and pedaling.

Cyndi was partially deaf, but it never got in her way of hammering up the trail and making the most out of life. She often wouldn't hear me when I spoke to her as we rode unless I yelled. She would check in for a rest and water break when we could talk more easily. Cyndi struggled with hearing the thunder, so I would alert her at the slightest rumble. I'm terrified of being outside in a thunderstorm. (I'm convinced lightning must have struck and killed me in another life.) I'm content sitting on my couch with a cup of tea and an inspirational book while a thunderstorm rages outside, but when I'm outside and the sky grows ominous, get me out of there! I want no part of it. If I get caught outside in a storm, I'm like a gazelle who suddenly finds itself in the den of a lion. I'm sure I have the same look of horror in my eyes. Often, we would need to descend down the trail before we could get to safety. Cyndi would continue to keep her cool and ever-so-calmly repeat her usual advice, "Keep on pedaling and don't freak out, Jill, we're fine."

In life, similar to biking, I know I can get through almost anything if I heed those words. Over the years of mountain biking, I've learned skills that have helped me navigate the technical sections. I think back to when I first started riding and how much harder it was to get through those sections before I had the skills I have now.

Cyndi died tragically on June 10, 2019, in a sudden mountain biking accident, just shy of her 69th birthday. Her death devastated the town. Cyndi was a Park City institution. She inspired and impacted me greatly. I wish I'd told her when she was here. Little did Cyndi know, she not only taught me how to be a better biker, but she also taught me about life and inspired me to write a book. Pedaling is the key to rolling a bike over any terrain. This so perfectly translates into our daily lives when dealing with Sticky Situations. We need to remember to grow our skills to be able to go steadily forward, even in the difficult times when we want to give up or quit.

May you rest in peace, Cyndi.

INTRODUCTION

We all find ourselves in tough situations sometimes. These issues come in many forms, but what they have in common is that they're hard to resolve or they require you to deal with a person who's unruly or hard to manage.

In this book, we're going to call any situation like this that you might encounter a "Sticky Situation." These can be anything from a co-worker who has bad body odor to one of your employees who dresses inappropriately for the work environment to an elderly neighbor you really care about but is asking too much of your time.

We all know that person with the issue no one wants to address. We sometimes go so far as acting like kids and play the "Not it!" game (think finger on the side of the nose) or hot potato game where no one wants to address the problem. You know what this does? It results in the issue never getting addressed. I'm willing to bet you've found yourself in a difficult situation like one of these. I know I sure have. Many times. Perhaps you're a manager at work and need to address something with an employee. When you try to address it, you get nervous and clam up because you either don't know how to put the right words together, you lack training on handling these types of situations, or you're worried about hurting someone's feelings. Maybe you've noticed the issue yourself and have been telling yourself you need to say something, but the thought of broaching the topic makes the bottom of your feet sweat. (Yes, this is a thing.)

Many of us become adults and realize no one ever taught us how to have these "Sticky Conversations." It's like when we grow up and leave the house and are expected to somehow know how to balance a checkbook and manage our finances. If you were one of the lucky ones taught these life skills, you're ahead of the pack. Similar to learning my finances, I've learned to handle Sticky Situations by basically just figuring out what has and hasn't worked until I realized I was doing the same thing every time . . . and it was working!

When we don't address Sticky Situations, they have the potential to cause never-ending arguments that drain us or, even worse, broken relationships. Failing to address Sticky Situations in the workplace can cause dysfunctional ongoing work relationships and lack of team collaboration. Lack of team cohesion results in decreased productivity and, often, a hit to the bottom line. Or, in your personal life, it may be the neighbor who's always asking for favors or borrows money and never pays it back. Maybe it's the obnoxious relative no one wants to invite to family gatherings because of their vocal political views or foul language when they drink. Maybe it's the guy with the body odor or the hostess who's wearing a revealing shirt in the restaurant.

Let's face it—we can't avoid Sticky Situations. They seem to pop up when we least expect. They consume us until we get them resolved. They rear their ugly heads like a new pimple on prom night. And, since you can't avoid them, it's important to hone your skills for dealing with them. Whether you want to address issues at work or in your personal life, this book can teach you how to face these situations head-on.

My five-step formula and three-prong simple, straightforward, and human-centered approach will prepare you to handle Sticky Situations of all kinds, instead of living in a state of constant avoidance or fear. I'll teach you to navigate the examples in this section and many more. Don't worry, it's easier than you think. After you conquer your first Sticky Situation, you'll be on a path for better collaboration and relationships in your life. Welcoming conflict and difficult situations and addressing them in a healthy way can open doors for innovation and alternative ways of doing things once you conquer the Sticky Situation.

The principles I'm going to teach you aren't novel. What I've done is synthesize ideas so they work together to produce resolutions to Sticky Situations. It's the combination of the steps and the three-prong approach that make them so effective.

This approach works. That said, I caution you about diving into these tactics without a prior relationship with the person you're having the conversation with, but don't panic if you haven't done the work to build the relationship. The way I have you address Sticky Situations will aid in building these relationships as you handle the situation. There won't always be an opportunity to build trust or a relationship first. In most situations, there are opportunities. Don't be fake and rush to do insincere things to build the relationship only to address the Sticky Situation a few days later. Like a bent valve in the engine of your Chevrolet, this approach will probably backfire.

In this book, you will learn:

- Five simple steps for handling Sticky Situations
- Personal development principles to further guide you
- You Got This! exercises to implement what you learn
- Game-Changing Personal Development Challenges
- [BONUS] My personal morning routine to get you

centered, productive, and ready to go out and conquer
your next Sticky Situation

I dedicate a chapter to each part of the approach to the five
steps. You may notice some overlap in the simple,
straightforward, and human-centered chapters. This is
intentional. To be most effective in dealing with Sticky
Situations, you'll need to tap into all three in some capacity. You
may rely on one piece more than another depending on the
situation, but by the end of the book, using the You Got This!
exercises at the end of each chapter, you will have outlined a
plan to address whatever Sticky Situation is weighing on you
right now.

I even walk you through some "What if?" scenarios. Listing the
"What ifs" has been immensely beneficial to my clients. At first,
they wonder why I take the time to discuss these hypotheticals,
but then when one happens, they are forever grateful. Even if
you don't predict a certain outcome, it always pays to have a
plan.

As a bonus, I've included my signature "Get the Wiggles Out"
morning routine as the last chapter of this book. I'm extremely
excited to share this with you. I love creating toolboxes of
information, so I figured it was only fitting to leave you with an
awesome tool you can use to reflect on and practice what you
learn—and help you focus each day with intentionality!

WHO THIS BOOK IS FOR

This book will be especially valuable to you if you work in HR,
own a business, or supervise others. It will also be beneficial if
you're living the human experience like the rest of us and want
tools to better navigate Sticky Situations in your life. This book
is for you if you want to dive in and get those Sticky Situations

resolved sooner than later and are open to growth and developing yourself personally along the way.

If you're searching for a silver bullet, keep in mind that there's no such thing. I'm not here to tell you this book will eliminate sleepless nights, headaches, and anxiety over dealing with a Sticky Situation, but employing the tactics can alleviate those stressors. While my approach is easy to implement, getting the exact result you want isn't always easy.

This book won't tell you when to and when not to address a Sticky Situation. You should listen to yourself to form the best decision about when the time is right to address it. This book also won't describe every possible scenario that could happen after you initially address the issue. You may need to seek further support to bring the issue to its final resolution. What I am offering is a novel way of thinking, and while it doesn't happen overnight, you'll get the hang of it in no time with some practice.

I'm sure you've heard the familiar adage that insanity is doing the same thing over and over and expecting different results. I know your way isn't working. (No. I'm not psychic. You gave it away when you picked up this book.) You can't keep trying the same techniques that aren't getting you anywhere. You need a fresh approach to conquering Sticky Situations. I'm here to show you the way.

This New Englander is wickedly excited to share this book with you. I truly hope you enjoy reading, have a few giggles, and feel empowered, motivated, and prepared to go out in the world and conquer the Sticky Situation weighing on you right now.

Footnotes will appear at the end of each chapter.

MY BACKGROUND

"Don't forget to check the oil!" my dad hollered as he jogged down the road after me, waving goodbye as I drove off in my brand-new Subaru sedan. It was a scene right out of the Dixie Chicks song, "Wide Open Spaces." I could see my mom's face wrinkle as she tried to hold back tears while she blew me a kiss from behind the classic New England screen door of the front porch. This Subaru was my first car, packed to the gills with my worldly possessions, my skis and bike strapped to the top. It looked like I was a member of the Clampett family. Despite having a fully capable sport rack, my dad had strapped and stretched a half a dozen yellow and red Bungee cords across the rack. We snaked them across and over my skis and bike. I was Utah-bound!

I itched for the wide-open big mountain terrain I read about in Ski magazine and the famous powder snow Utah is famous for. Chills ran up my spine the moment I saw the Rocky Mountains rise up toward the sky in front of me as I drove closer to Park City. This was where I belonged!

Over the next 20 years, I did it all in Human Resources. I worked in the HR trenches entering data, I built and managed

HR teams of all sizes, and I held a seat at the strategic table. I worked in Human Resources roles across the hospitality, technology, and medical device industries. I experienced everything from rapid growth environments and global mergers and acquisitions to mass layoffs and business closures—and believe me, there were many, many Sticky Situations in between! I undertook every opportunity and challenge head-on and was hungry to extract all the knowledge and expertise I could from every experience. This brings me to today where I now own an HR Consulting company, Expedition HR.

I jump out of bed each morning. (You laugh, but I do. I'm the ultimate morning person. *Hello, 5:00 a.m.*!) I start the day feeling energized and excited about my work, thankful for all my opportunities, successes, and failures. (Yes, you heard that right. The failures are where I've learned the most in my life.) I'm proud to officially call myself an HR nerd—I mean, expert.

I don't have all the answers, but I do have expertise I'd like to share. I hope to do it in a way that will be beneficial, enlightening . . . and, most important, fun to read! If we can't have a little fun in our work, what's the point?

FIVE STEPS TO CONQUERING STICKY SITUATIONS

S o, you're finally ready to stop living in a state of avoidance. You're determined to tell your neighbor that she's making the entire neighborhood uncomfortable when she gets undressed in front of her window. But how to even start?

I've created five steps that are the foundation for acing any type of Sticky Situation conversation. If you're ready to face these difficult conversations head-on, these steps are crucial; they'll teach you the exact format of how to craft your message and get your ideas out so you can articulate exactly what you want to say and leave no room for misinterpretation.

Applying this format and factoring in the tips from the successive chapters will ensure that the point you're trying to get across is clear, crisp, and effective.

Layered on to this five-step formula is my three-prong simple, straightforward, and human-centered approach. The combination of the five steps and the approach is the key to conquering Sticky Situations!

. . .

THIS FIVE-STEP PROCESS WILL HELP YOU:

- Stay focused
- Be direct
- Be concise

Before we dive into the five steps, I want to note that I advocate addressing "Sticky Conversations" sooner than later. That said, the right preparation is also essential. Once you bring the issue into the open, you can't take it back. Be clear on why it's important to you to address the issue. Maybe you need to get something off your chest, or maybe you need to see improvements in a certain area. But identifying your ultimate goal will help guide you in how you approach the matter.

It's also important to know when you shouldn't bring up a conversation. One example may be if you've given your notice to quit your job and only have another week of work left. Addressing a Sticky Situation in your workplace may brew unnecessary tension for your last days. Conversely, in a workplace where you are invested for the long-term, it makes sense to address Sticky Situations. The best advice I can give is to use your best judgement. (See chapter 8, "Know When to Hold 'Em, Know When to Fold 'Em" for guidance.) To have or not have the difficult conversation isn't something I can teach you in this book, but I can teach you the five steps to use to address the issue at hand once you've decided you want to.

THE FIVE-STEP FORMULA

1. Thanks
2. Why
3. What
4. How
5. Thanks Again

THANKS

The first step is to express gratitude, which has a place everywhere, even in tough conversations . . . *especially* in tough conversations. (More about the importance of gratitude in chapter 4, "Prong Three—Human-Centered.")

Start with thanking the person you're talking to for having the conversation to begin with. Then, explain that you're bringing the topic up with them because:

- You care for them.
- You value your relationship (work or personal).
- They're valuable to your work team/social group, etc.

If none of the above fit the conversation or feel right to you, simply dive in and tell the person you need to have a tough conversation with them. You don't need to give thanks if it's more natural for you to say, "I need to have a tough conversation with you today." Another way to voice this is, "I need to bring up something with you that's going to be difficult to talk about. May I have your permission to do so?" When they give you permission, you can then thank them for being willing. You even have a blended option with this and one of the above. For example, "I need to bring up something with you that's going to be difficult to talk about. I'm doing it because our relationship is important to me, and I care about you." You may not want to ask if you can have the conversation, but if it feels better, do it. It is very rare that someone will not allow you to voice your concern. This tactic sets the stage for sharing something difficult. To say it's going to be a tough conversation can be a relief to both sides in some ways. Pause for a second. Then, go ahead with step two.

WHY

The second step is to state the reason for the difficult conversation. This is where you get the issue out into the open, address the elephant in the room as they say. After the breath you took after the opening thank-you statement, share the reason for the difficult conversation.

If you're at work and ending someone's employment, this is the time to deliver this news. "Susan, we're here because we're letting you go today." Boom.

Voice exactly what it is that you're asking that they stop doing and/or what you're asking for them to do. Sidestepping the issue is likely the whole reason this issue became sticky in the first place and now requires this difficult conversation.

Sometimes it works for you to combine the Thanks and Why steps, and they don't necessarily have to happen in that order. When we put the Thanks and Why steps together, it looks like this:

"Hi Sue, thanks for taking a minute to chat with me. I need to talk to you about borrowing my clothes. I care about our friendship and don't want this issue to cause tension."

WHAT

The third step, What, is to state exactly what needs to change. Don't dance around it. Elaborate on what you said in step 2, Why. The What should be short and to the point. Recall the goals of this process: stay focused, be direct, be concise. (We'll go into more detail on these in the successive chapters.)

There may only be one issue to address. If so, state the one issue. If there are multiple issues, perhaps at work if there are performance issues, I recommend you address no more than three at a time. Have another conversation later to address the additional issues. In your first conversation, focus on no more than the three most pressing issues.

An important note if you're addressing performance is to ensure you separate issues with performance from medical or personal issues. It is important not to muddy the waters. Address performance as a standalone. Address other factors in the situation separately. (See chapter 5, "What If?")

To revisit the borrowing clothes example, this step may sound like this: "You borrowed clothes from me four times in the last month. I'll share two instances, once when you borrowed my pink top and the other when you borrowed my gray pants. You returned them with stains. I had to pay a dry cleaner to get the stains out and felt frustrated about that."

How

The next step is to tell the person you're speaking with exactly how you expect the behavior to change or what you expect them to start or stop doing. At work, if you're having a performance discussion, tell them what they need to do to be successful and outline the specific consequences/outcomes for not changing the behavior. If you need to address something with a co-worker or perhaps your manager at work, you'll want to be clear on what behavior you're asking they change or the different way you ask that they treat you. In the two work situations mentioned here and the example with borrowing clothes, you will want to say what needs to happen to repair the issue or, as applicable, the consequences for not doing so.

Be clear on what determines resolution of the issues you discussed. You should have a system for follow-up in place before you have this conversation at work. This prevents you having this conversation without a solid process for adequate follow-up to ensure the requested change or changes take place.

In a work performance situation, I recommend asking a question after you note what needs to change, such as, "Do you agree to change these things I shared to reach the outcome we need?"

With a termination of employment, or if you need to sever a relationship through this conversation, just express thanks again for having the conversation. That is sufficient. You need not ask if they agree to make the requested improvement because the relationship is ending. Since there's nothing to change and you already shared the outcome, there's no need to follow up or tell them "how" you ask that they improve. In this case, asking "Do you have questions?" at the end is a good way to close. (See more in chapter 5, "What If?" which shares what you can do if they keep asking questions and/or want more detail in a termination.)

In this clothing example, this step may sound like this: "I'm happy to continue to lend you clothes on occasion, but ask you to check for stains before returning them. If they have stains, please take them to the dry cleaner before returning them to me."

THANKS AGAIN

This part is simple. Tell them again that you appreciate that they had the conversation with you.

The example about borrowing clothes may sound like this with all five steps included:

"Hi Sue, thanks for taking a minute to chat with me. I need to talk to you about borrowing my clothes. I care about our friendship and don't want this issue to cause tension. You borrowed clothes from me four times in the last month. I'll share two instances, once when you borrowed my pink top and the other when you borrowed my gray pants. You returned them with stains. I had to pay a dry cleaner to get the stains out and felt frustrated about that. I'm happy to continue to lend you clothes on occasion, but ask you to check for stains before returning them. If they have stains, please take them to the dry cleaner before returning to me. Thanks for being open to having this conversation. I value our relationship and know we can move past this."

BODY LANGUAGE ESSENTIALS FOR STICKY CONVERSATIONS

There are many ways you can use body language to your advantage to aid the words you use in a Sticky Conversation. These will help you be most effective.

These essentials are:

- *Eye Contact:* Make "gentle" eye contact, which means keeping the other person's gaze for a few seconds at a time. (Don't make it a staring contest!)
- *Hand placement:* Depending on where you are having the conversation, either set your hands on the table in front of you in a natural way (clasped together is a good option), or rest your hands in your lap or on your knees or thighs. Choose which feels most natural to you. Try it out in front of a mirror when you practice your message and see what feels best. You can switch positions if needed during the conversation, but avoid moving too much because that can make you appear nervous or anxious.
- *Sloooooow it down*: Speak slowly and articulate your words.

- *Breathe/Summon Calm:* Breathe before you speak as well as during the conversation to keep you feeling calm and collected with your message.

When you employ these types of "positive" body language, it bolsters your message. It also helps you avoid sending confusing signals when your message says one thing and your body language says another.

FLEXIBILITY

There may be times when you may not use all the steps based on the details of the situation, since each situation is unique. I still encourage you to familiarize yourself with each step as a basis for preparing for conversations. You can always take out what you don't need. Taking the time to prepare will ensure that you use all the steps that are applicable. Don't get so attached to each step that you can't forge ahead with the conversation toward the desired outcome. The point of the steps is to ease stress, and not create it. Do what feels right while using these steps as a guideline.

WHAT'S NEXT?

In the next three chapters, I'll guide you through the process of incorporating simple, straightforward, and human-centered approaches into this five-step formula.

In chapter 7, I'll tie it all together with examples that incorporate all the pieces.

As my daughter, Jenna (age 7), told me when she found out I was writing this book, "You need to always be eating a donut when you have a Sticky Conversation." I don't know about you, but I think this is excellent advice!

2

PRONG ONE—SIMPLIFY

The first prong of the three-prong approach is to simplify. Or as I like to call it, "Less said, best said." The clearest message is one with few words and the most impact. Forgetting to keep things simple risks the entire message going off track.

Raise your hand if you want to complicate your life!

Who wants to add mental and physical stress to each day?

Who likes a cluttered mind and space?

It sounds silly for me to even ask these questions. The interesting thing is most would answer no, yet they don't operate simply in their work or in their personal lives. We often produce situations and choices that are much more complex than necessary. I'm here to take you through ways to simplify at work and in other areas of your life . . . especially in Sticky Conversations.

Simple means keeping the message short. Those who get their message across best rarely need to use fancy words or long-winded monologues to make a point. The simpler the message, the more it will resonate with others. Simplifying makes it easier for the audience—a live audience, email audience, or the person sitting in front of you—to digest the information.

In order to keep the message short, a rule of thumb is to set a time frame for a Sticky Conversation. If the conversation goes longer than the time frame you set, plan to stop and revisit later so as not to do more harm than good. Set a later time (either later in the day or in the next day or two) when you'll continue and finish the conversation. This serves to give all parties time to reflect on what was discussed and perhaps think of solutions on their own, which may help ensure the next conversation leads to a resolution.

In Sticky Conversations, try and always keep this acronym I created for SIMPLE in your mind:

- S = Short
- I = Informative
- M = Meaningful
- P = Poignant
- L = Lean
- E = Emphasis

I LOVE SIMPLICITY

I get up at 5:00 a.m. To me, mornings are the most special time of the day. Having this as one of my non-negotiable habits simplifies my life. (Through my "Get the WIGGLES Out" morning routine, which I share in the last chapter of this book, you too can experience the magic of a morning routine!) My mornings give me the mental space to simplify what I have going on and focus on the most important action items for the day. This habit puts me in the right state of mind to tackle the challenges that come up in the day. (Check out James Clear's book, *Atomic Habits*, to learn more about the process he outlines to either create or break a habit.)

It's easier for me to have a simple, easy-to-follow, non-negotiable morning routine than for each day to be different. I like to be in control. I keep things in control by keeping things simple.

Simplicity in my life gives me order and mental calm. I dislike extra stuff lying around. What I keep is intentional. I focus on my favorite things which "give me joy." (If this idea of living minimally interests you, check out Marie Kondo's book, *The Life-Changing Magic of Tidying Up*.) Simplifying at its best!

Why the rant about my magic mornings, habits, and being a minimalist? I want to model this point: simple means less clutter to sift through physically and less clutter in your mental space. Simplicity in handling Sticky Conversations makes sense, so we don't fall into the trap of saying too much and clouding the message we worked so hard to prepare. Therefore, minimizing the number of words is essential in each of the five steps to handling Sticky Situations.

EXERCISE: SIMPLE PREPARATION

Preparation is key to ensuring the intended message is simple and to the point. As part of your preparation for Why, step 2 of the five-step process, set aside 15 minutes to go through the simplifying process outlined below.

1. *Quiet Brainstorm:* Pick a time when you can be alone. Set a timer for five to ten minutes and type or write all the things on your mind bothering you about this Sticky Situation. Write everything, no matter how trivial or how big the issues seem. A big list is fine. It's ok if there are similar issues phrased different ways. The idea here is to get everything written down.
2. *Brainstorm Review:* When the timer ends, review the list. Circle repeated themes that fall under the same overarching issue.

3. *Final Themes:* Compile a new list of the themes you found, being sure to merge those which were repeated themes. If this list has more than three themes, decide which are the most concerning one to three topics to bring up. If needed, repeat steps one and two to narrow the themes down to a maximum of three. I suggest limiting yourself to three issues because bringing up a never-ending list of grievances is not a productive way to improve things. You risk making the other person feel discouraged and unhappy if you bring up too much at once. Rather than focusing on improving a few things, they may get confused and upset about there being so many things to address.

4. *Summarize Final Themes:* Write one sentence summing up each of the issues you uncovered. Write exactly what the issues are, so there is no way to misinterpret. Don't be vague. I recommend writing this in whatever form it comes to mind and then going back and taking out words so your message is short, simple, and straight to the point. (You will learn more about getting your words to a minimum later in this chapter in the section called "Script, Then Remove.") Call to mind supporting examples. Doing this confirms you have solid reasons to address your issues. I never recommend charging ahead into a Sticky Conversation unless you have solid examples to support the issues being addressed. This is especially true if you're addressing an issue at work. In a court of law, it's hard to prove a case when you have no facts. Same idea applies here.

During step 2, "Brainstorm Review," notice if you've come up with a seemingly never-ending list of grievances or issues. If you have, consider why you're trying to save the relationship in the first place. In a work situation, this might apply to someone who has many serious performance issues. Perhaps it makes more sense to part ways than waste time and resources trying to resolve all the issues. (There is a full script for this type of scenario in chapter 7, "Tying It All Together.") If it's important to preserve the relationship, you'll want to take time to address these things gradually and address the most pressing issue first. You can always revisit other issues later. Often, after you do this list work, you'll find all the topics can be boiled down to just a couple key issues.

RUN-ON SENTENCES

We're all guilty of using run-on sentences at one point or another. Run-on sentences cause the listener/reader to get lost. The lack of simplicity obscures the sentence's intended focus. Later in this chapter, I'll teach you about scripting and removing. Don't worry about run-on sentences when you write your initial script. In the brainstorming phase, it's important to write things as they come to mind, even if they're run-ons. Later, you will remove the fluff or unnecessary parts and eliminate run-on sentences.

REPETITION

I love this one. Repeat yourself if you need to once you've said your piece. Repeating keeps you from saying something unplanned which can result in the conversation going off track. It can also keep you from muddying the waters or even causing a legal situation in the workplace. (I'll elaborate on this in chapter 3, "Prong Two—Tell It to 'Em Straight.") Repetition is especially helpful in Sticky Conversations. When you've taken the time to plan what you will say, the last thing you want to happen is for unplanned issues to be introduced to the conversation. Remember, the purpose of the steps is to keep you focused. Perhaps you're a manager and must fire someone, and they want to dispute your reasoning. They rant on and on about the ways you've done them wrong. Repetition is a must in these situations to ensure you stick to your script and don't get yourself into hot water by uttering something you will regret. In life, you risk ruining a friendship or relationship by bringing up something unplanned and opening a can of worms.

REFINING THE SCRIPT

Script, Then Remove

As you go through the five steps, I recommend starting with a "brain-dump." That's when you just put all your thoughts into a first draft, using the steps in the preparation at the beginning of this chapter. Then, go back and remove and/or replace words to be more concise and to reach a final script. Follow these steps:

Script: Set a timer for 10 minutes. Write out your thoughts in whatever way comes to you initially—even if it's raw, obnoxious, and brutally honest. Let your emotions hang out in this step. It's okay if it's wordy, messy, and not well-written. Write out everything that comes to mind about the situation. If you get stuck, refer to the preparation process from earlier in this chapter to jog your thoughts.

Remove: Review what you put together and ensure you have everything included from the five steps to handling Sticky Conversations.

Disaster Clean-Up

Clean up the words: Make sure the words you use aren't attacking or mean. We're all human and it is common to have emotion around Sticky Situations and those emotions may show up as you write your script.

Eliminate filler words: A filler word is any meaningless word or phrase used during speech to fill silence. Some examples of filler words are: *just, that, very, really, totally, due to the fact that,* and *actually*. These words do (actually) have a time and a place but I find, when I write, 90% of the time they can (really) simply be removed and (that) the sentence sounds (just) fine without them. Get my point? (You will find few of these words in this book. This was intentional because my goal was to state things simply and not dilute my message. I do my best to practice what I preach!) You can search for and replace or delete those filler words—most likely delete them. Take out those darned *buts* and *howevers*. (You will learn more about taking out the *buts* and *howevers* in the next chapter.) Rewrite or shorten run-on sentences. Insert periods and start new thoughts instead of run-ons. You'll quickly see how fast it cleans up your message.

Final Review: Review what you have left after your disaster clean-up. If time remains, run your final version by someone you respect who will give you honest feedback and helpful suggestions. Ask them if your message is clear or confusing.

Memorize: Once you have the issues simplified, memorize them. If you have trouble memorizing them, they're too long and you need to go back and edit again. You want to articulate these points in their simplest form when you have the Sticky Conversation.

Here is an example of a first draft when you're planning an employee termination:

> Thanks for meeting with me. We're here today because we're letting you go from the company. We appreciate the work performed over your seven years of employment and know this isn't easy to hear. Your performance has not improved after a first and second warning. Another reason we're letting you go is your attendance. You have also been absent 32 of the last 90 days. When you're absent from work, others are saddled with the extra work. This causes morale to go down and can be frustrating to the rest of the team. We all need time away from

work, but when it gets excessive, it becomes a problem. We understand it happens sometimes. I want to thank you again for the work you've done for us. You were instrumental in helping us build the department and complete key projects. I have your final check and termination paperwork here, which details your benefits as you end employment. Do you have questions? We want to thank you again for the work you did and we wish you the best.

Here is the marked-up version:

Thanks for meeting with me. We're here today because we're letting you go ~~from the company~~. We appreciate the work you did for us. ~~performed over your seven years of employment and know this isn't easy to hear.~~ Your performance has not improved after a first and second warning. ~~performance.~~ ~~Another reason we're letting you go is your attendance.~~ You've been absent 32 of the last 90 days. When you're absent ~~from work~~, others are saddled with ~~the~~ extra work. This ~~causes morale to go down and can be~~ is frustrating to ~~the rest of~~ the team. W~~e all need time away from work, but when it gets excessive it becomes a problem. We understand it happens sometimes. I want to~~ Thank you again for ~~the work you've done for us. You were instrumental in~~ helping us build the department and complete key projects. I have your final check and termination paperwork here, which details your benefits as you end employment. Do you have questions? We want to thank you again. ~~for the work you did and~~ We wish you the best.

Clear and concise message left:

Thanks for meeting with me. We're here today because we're letting you go. We appreciate the work you did for us. Your performance hasn't improved after a first and second warning.

You've been absent 32 of the last 90 days. When you're absent, others are saddled with extra work. This is frustrating to the team. Thank you again for helping us build the department and complete key projects. I have your final check and termination paperwork here, which details your benefits as you end employment. Do you have questions? We want to thank you again. We wish you the best.

Clients sometimes ask, "Won't it sound fake or canned?" My response: "Wouldn't it be worth it to sound scripted rather than you missing the mark with your message in the first place?" Food for thought!

THREE "SIMPLIFY" NUGGETS

- Beware of run-on sentences, and losing the focus of the conversation.
- Repeat yourself instead of sharing new or additional information.
- Utilize the "Script, Then Remove" process to "brain dump," and then refine what you'll say.

RECAP

Using fewer words and repeating one simple message sets you up for a more successful Sticky Conversation. It leaves less room for misinterpretation and more room for the most important things. Using fewer words goes hand in hand with simplifying your message.

YOU GOT THIS! LET'S PRACTICE . . .

Get your free PDF supplemental workbook at
conquerstickysituations.com/workbook

In this exercise, I'd like for you to think of a specific Sticky Situation either at work or in your personal life. This can be one that is present now, one from the past, or something you foresee becoming "sticky." Once you've identified your Sticky Situation, take these steps:

1. Do the "Simple Preparation" outlined in this chapter.
2. Read what you have out loud. How does the message make you feel? Does it feel natural? Is it direct and clear with no room for misinterpretation? (It may feel awkward at first because you're doing something new and using fewer words than you are accustomed to.)

The exercises in the next chapter will build on what you created here.

PERSONAL DEVELOPMENT CHALLENGE

I challenge you to use the skills you learned about simplicity not just for preparing for Sticky Situations, but also in your everyday life. When you have everyday conversations, think how you can plan your words to be succinct and to the point. When you have a Sticky Situation to address, simplifying your message will then feel like second nature.

3

PRONG TWO—TELL IT TO 'EM STRAIGHT

The second prong to layer on top of the five-step process is pretty straightforward. Really. That's it; it's straightforward. You not only need to keep your message simple and short, but you also need to be direct and to the point. A brief, but vague message is useless.

AM I STRAIGHTFORWARD . . . OR BRUTALLY HONEST?

Straightforward applies not only to the manner of addressing something or getting one's point across. It also means being transparent—not brutally honest—regular honest. It also relates to boundaries, but we'll get into that later. I'll start with defining straightforward as it relates to addressing Sticky Situations and being upfront with what you say.

We humans dislike uncertainty. When we have information, even information other than what we're hoping to hear, we often feel better about a situation. It can leave us feeling more empowered to control our actions.

"I'm brutally honest. It's who I am."

I'll share an example I experienced in the workplace years ago. There was a manager, who we'll call Sally, who acted unprofessionally towards her leadership team peers. Sally frequently criticized the way her peers performed various aspects of their jobs, such as the way they set their team goals, their work schedules, and the ways they tracked their team progress. Sally insisted that her way was the right way because of her number of years' experience in the field.

To address the issue, I shared with Sally what was brought to my attention about the situation, specifically how other managers perceived her words and actions. I asked Sally if she understood the concerns, how her behavior was being perceived, and the things which needed to change. I told her that I wanted to know if she had any ideas on ways to rectify the issue.

Sally's eyes darted to the picture on the wall beside where we were sitting as she acknowledged she doesn't always handle these interactions as well as she could. I could see a tension form in her face and posture as she went on to say, "Well, I'm brutally honest. It's who I am. I will not apologize for who I am." I saw the same tone and body language she likely displayed with the managers who complained.

I responded, "I respect who you are as a person. I would never try to change who you or anyone else is as a person." After a momentary pause, I said, "The way you communicate gives the perception of a lack of professionalism. Other people's perceptions are tough because, whether we believe them or not, they're there. At work, being brutally honest as you described yourself, or too abrupt or defensive, has the potential to inhibit your chances of advancement here and even your professional growth." (Notice, I did *not* use the words "but" or "however" after I told her I respect her as a person. We'll come back to that.) I paused again. I wanted to see what she thought of what I said.

She responded with, "Well, it is who I am." Unfortunately Sally never realized how her version of being straightforward through being "brutally honest" wasn't the path to success for her at the company.

There's a difference between being professionally direct (a.k.a. straightforward) and "brutally honest" like Sally. Being straightforward means relaying the message in a way that's easily understood and right to the point. It describes the ability to communicate in an assertive and direct, yet professional, way.

BALANCING STRAIGHTFORWARDNESS AND TACT

Being straightforward is tricky because it entails speaking the truth and reality of a situation, while maintaining professionalism and being transparent without exposing confidential information. It is *not* beating around the bush about the truth. It means not using too many words and padding the message with irrelevant information. I often talk to clients about a situation and tell them, "The reality is . . ." This is often how I lead into telling them something in this straightforward manner I describe here. People often ask me how they can balance being straightforward when asked a question, while protecting the company's information. The answer is, tell them what you know and are able to share with them. Then tell them what you can't tell them. This approach addresses the fact openly that you can't tell them certain things. In this situation, that *is* being straightforward and transparent. Are you going to please everyone with this approach? No. Even when done in the right way, being straightforward won't please everyone, but this book isn't about pleasing everyone; it's about succeeding at Sticky Conversations.

How do you feel when you receive an email one-liner such as, "Where are you with the report?" To me, this is very off-putting. If you want to earn respect, being rude and overly direct isn't the way to earn it, nor is it how you build relationships. Here are a few ways to find a balance between applying humanity and being straightforward, which facilitates getting what you need out of the conversation.

EXAMPLES: ASKING FOR OVERDUE WORK

What you want to say: "Where's the TPS report? It's now Tuesday, and it was due last Thursday!"

Try replacing with: "Hi Steve, I hope you had a restful weekend. I'm checking in to see if there is an update on the TPS report from last week. You typically turn things in on time, so I wanted to ensure things were okay. It is important that you complete the report today."

～

What you want to say: "You never get things done on time. You need to be micro-managed, so I'm checking in to ensure that you're on track with the upcoming deadline."

Try replacing with: "Hello Roger, I hope you had a good evening with your family. How are things going along with the project? Perhaps I can set up some time for us to meet, and we can review what you've put together and assess whether the project is on track?"

I encourage you to be a leader by taking the approach of having a conversation as two humans rather than one person with a strict agenda demanding something from another.

Please, please, please (Yes, I *am* begging you) avoid saying or writing the following No-No phrases. They're off-putting and rude. No one likes to hear these things, and they often put the receiver on the defensive.

- As I mentioned already . . .
- Per my other email . . .
- As I already/previously stated . . .
- Like I said . . .

THREE STEPS TO BEING MORE STRAIGHTFORWARD

To be straightforward, I encourage you to do these things:

1. *Plan:* Take the needed time to think about how you'll relay the message and the exact desired outcome.
2. *Think Simple:* Remember, less said, best said. Be brief. Be direct. Be professional and kind.
3. *Practice:* Instill these skills as a part of who you are instead of only who you are at work. When you practice this approach in all areas of your life, you'll see results everywhere. It will be easier to remember this approach when you're at work if you intentionally make it something you commit to in your personal life.

Asking straightforward and pertinent questions is one way to open the Sticky Conversation. Start with having people reflect on answers to questions you ask. Try to avoid yes and no questions. You also want to avoid asking questions which can solicit a grunt or a monosyllabic "fine." (Shudder. I'm having a premonition of my kids' teenage years.) Examples of questions or requests for information that will not yield a yes/no response are:

- What do you see as the biggest issues or concerns with this situation?
- What are some words you would use to describe the current work environment on your team?
- Please share something going well and something not going so well in your department.

There are laws which were enacted to basically ensure employers do not act like jerks and unjustly discriminate against someone for things over which the individual lacks control. Where employers go astray is to take no action toward an individual if they fall into a protected class.[1] Some employers go so far as to not explore the performance issues, for fear of a misstep and getting sued solely because that person may be a certain age or a certain nationality. This isn't the right approach either. In fact, this is a great opportunity to be straightforward. Don't misunderstand me. I'm completely opposed to treating individuals adversely because they fall into one of the protected classes under Title VII. Absolutely. By the same token, an employer shouldn't halt efforts to correct performance if the employee falls into one of these protected classes purely for fear of legal repercussions. There is a right and wrong way to go about this.

Employers have a responsibility to flesh out the work-related reason for the performance issue. Once this due diligence is complete, the employer should feel confident in addressing the performance issues in a straightforward manner and taking appropriate action.[2]

It pains me to see workplaces with underperforming employees in either the wrong position or not performing adequately in their current position. It also troubles me to see employers who are in a constant state of avoidance in addressing performance issues because they're unclear how to gather the right facts and be straightforward about what is going on in the situation.

PRACTICE, PRACTICE, PRACTICE!

Once you figure out your straightforward message for your Sticky Situation, practice it. Practice it out loud! Repeat it until you are comfortable saying it. Do it in front of a mirror making eye contact with yourself. See what your face does when you say it. Try it out with a partner. Going into a Sticky Situation and trying to vocalize your opening straightforward sentence for the first time out loud won't feel good at all. Don't skip this step. Similar to how repetition is a tool for keeping the message simple, practice is a great tool for being straightforward.

ELIMINATE BUTS AND HOWEVERS

Watch out for two sneaky words that can ruin your Sticky Situation message. *But* and *However.* Separating your thoughts into two distinct sentences is a way to ensure one doesn't unintentionally negate the other. When you want to use one of these unnecessary words, stick a big period in there and end the sentence.

Start a new sentence with the thought that was going to appear after the *but* or *however.* Once you remove those words, you may need to make small edits to make the new sentences flow. It may feel awkward at first, but it'll feel more normal the more you do it. It will become a habit. You'll start noticing when you want to use these words, and will hopefully refer back to this technique of how to remove them.

EXAMPLES: REMOVING BUTS AND HOWEVERS FROM YOUR SENTENCES

BUT

Before: You're great with our customers and they give rave reviews about your follow up and customer service on the phone, but there's an issue with you missing deadlines.

After: You're great with our customers. They give rave reviews about your follow up and customer service on the phone. I wanted to talk with you today about missing recent deadlines.

～

Before: You're such a good listener and I value our friendship, but lately I feel like you don't listen and are constantly checking your phone whenever we're together.

After: You're such a good listener and I value our friendship. Lately, I feel like you don't listen and are constantly checking your phone when we're together.

HOWEVER

Before: I can tell you value your work because I see you here early each morning; however, I'm concerned about your relationship with your team.

After: I can tell you value your work because I see you here early each morning. We're meeting today to discuss some concerns with your relationship with your team.

～

Before: You are learning to dribble the soccer ball much better than you did at the start of the season; however, the last two games you have been kicking the ball when you are too far from the goal, when you should have dribbled further down the field, causing the ball to go out of bounds.

After: Your dribbling has improved so much since the start of the season! To avoid the ball going out of bounds, let's work on timing when you should keep dribbling down the field versus when you make a bigger kick.

Removing these words isn't an easy habit to change. Next time you're speaking with someone, simply note when you use them. Be aware of when you use them. Note what happens to the sentence when these words appear. Then, try to be intentional about eliminating them. Start new sentences where appropriate.

This is especially important if you're a manager and regularly give feedback. Be sure you don't give a compliment and immediately negate it by inserting a *but* or *however.*

Think of using *buts* and *howevers* in Sticky Conversations as similar to using compliment sandwiches. I despise compliment sandwiches as much as I hate mayonnaise when it's snuck into my ham sandwich. For those of you who don't know what a compliment sandwich is, it's when you deliver a piece of feedback but try and disguise it between two compliments. This may seem like a good idea, but the compliments end up sounding fake and insincere to the recipient. They make the feedback anything but straightforward.

APOLOGIES AND EXCUSES

Lady friends, listen up! Women say they're sorry more times in their lives than men. That's probably because men and women have differing ideas about what makes an action deserving of an apology, and I'm sorry to tell you that women have a lower threshold for the behavior they think warrants an apology.

Being straightforward is not a reason to apologize. This applies only if you're being straightforward in the right way, not the I'm-being-brutally-honest way and hurting someone with your words. You should not begin your straightforward statement with, "Sorry . . . but I need to have a tough conversation." No, no, no! While you're dropping the sorry, drop the "but" too. Do your preparation, and then dive in and address the thing . . . with confidence.

Having boundaries identifies the "yesses" and "nos" in your life. Standing up for yourself and your actions means you have boundaries, and that's something you should be proud of rather than something you should apologize for. Will everyone like these boundaries you set? Spoiler alert: You'll upset people when you're vocal about your boundaries, especially if you haven't been clear about your boundaries previously. The best way to teach others about healthy boundaries is to enforce yours! When we define boundaries at work and in our personal lives, we're straightforward about what we will and won't accept or tolerate. We know what those boundaries are in our hearts. The respect you earn over time as you continue to set your boundaries will amaze you.

A vital part of setting boundaries is not making excuses for them. Let me give some examples of what I mean. Let's pretend you have a boundary where you put your young kids to bed early. You're attending a family reunion, and your extended family is playing a game outside the rented vacation house near the firepit on a warm summer night. You tell your kids, "After you finish your game, it's time to head inside and get ready for bed." They don't talk back because they know the expectation. They understand the boundary you, their parent, set for them. Maybe you get some resistance by your cousin pleading, "Oh, let them stay up longer! They're on vacation!" This boundary is important to you because they need to get their rest so they're happy for the whole vacation. You respond, "They had so much fun. They'll see you all in the morning." This response is plenty. It confirms your boundary and simply restates what you previously stated using alternate words. Not only do you not need to give an excuse, but you also need not utter one sorry.

I'll give you a couple personal examples of my own boundaries. I prioritize taking vacations with my family and stepping fully away from work. I've built my business around being able to do this. Before vacations, I plan accordingly and get any work done before the trip. I arrange back-up support for my clients if they have something urgent come up in my absence. I communicate fully with my clients the details of when I'll be away and ensure they feel comfortable. Setting boundaries may not always be easy, but it's worth it since it can ensure that you're keeping the most important things to you sacred.

Why do we immediately think we need to give an excuse or give an elaborate reason for declining an invitation when we simply don't want to go? We sometimes think if we don't have a good reason, we better formulate one out of concern that the person inviting us will think less of us if we don't accept the invite. So many people overcommit themselves in their personal lives and end up miserable because they say yes to everything. What if you didn't need to feel mean or guilty when you·decline an invitation from a friend? What if you could decline in a straightforward and kind way that leaves everyone feeling good? You can!

It gets easier each time you do it. You'll soon see this become a habit in the way you respond. I speak from personal experience. Those with whom I've shared this technique observe that it gets easier and became a habit for them too. Before long, you'll decline invitations that don't serve you—with ease! Your calendar will be full of the right things that fill you up, rather than drain you.

You may ask, "Okay, so what if I want to give a reason, not an excuse?" There's a very fine, sometimes hardly noticeable, line between an excuse and a reason. You know, like the fine line between itching your nose versus picking it. Validate your boundary by adding something like, "We like to read to the kids before bed and getting rest is very important for kids, so we go to bed early." You can tell if this is a reason or an excuse by asking yourself if you're saying this to defend your boundary, or if it's truly helping support the straightforward way you're relaying information.

Here's what it sounds like to not use an excuse. A friend asks you to host a party for a multi-level marketing brand of cookware or jewelry. You want to support her, but this type of event gives you the heebie-jeebies to attend, never mind to host. As you call to mind what you learned in this book about being straightforward, composing your thoughts simply (using the five-step formula), and keeping your communication human-centered, you craft your response. "I appreciate you thinking of me. While I want to support you, I can't host a party. I am uncomfortable with hosting a multi-level marketing party. Is there something else I can do to support you?" If it's not genuine that you want to support them, skip the part where you offer to help them in another way. If you sincerely want to support them, but not in the way they requested, keep an open mind after you ask the question. Stick to your no for hosting a party but be willing to discuss other ways you can support as a good friend.

A nonideal response would be to say you can't host because of a schedule conflict. You're apologizing, making up an excuse, and not drawing a clear boundary that you're not interested in hosting the party. All you've done is open a window for them to propose another date. You're right back where you started. You even made it more awkward for yourself and perpetuated the stickiness because now you have to say no *again*. You may feel like you need to share another excuse when you could have been straightforward initially and gotten to the end result sooner.

EXAMPLES: DECLINE AN INVITATION OR WORK MEETING WITHOUT APOLOGIZING (OR SOUNDING LIKE A JERK!)

What not to say: "You're always booking meetings on top of my other meetings!"

Try replacing with: "Holding this meeting is important. I have a conflict at the time you suggested. Does a time between 1 p.m. and 3 p.m. work for you?"

～

What not to say: "I'm never available on Fridays for a late lunch—you should know this! Can't we do it another day?"

Try replacing with: "Monday through Thursday is ideal for me for a later lunch. I can be available anytime from 1 p.m. to 5 p.m. any of those days if something in there works. Thanks for your flexibility and for working with my schedule."

~

What not to say: "We should brainstorm via email instead of having these annoying marathon meetings. The last thing we need is *another* inefficient meeting!"

Try replacing with: "It is top priority to find a suitable solution. Perhaps if each of us presents some initial brainstormed options through email, we can come together at a later time and have a short, efficient meeting."

THREE "TELL IT TO 'EM STRAIGHT" NUGGETS

- Eliminate *buts* and *howevers.*
- There is no need for an excuse or an apology for being straightforward.
- Set clear boundaries and watch how you earn respect.

RECAP

In this chapter, you learned you can apply being straightforward to your life by setting firm boundaries and communicating them —no excuses needed! There's no reason to apologize for being straightforward when you do it in the right way. Using fewer words and being straightforward with those few words is essential for handling Sticky Conversations.

YOU GOT THIS! LET'S PRACTICE . . .

This exercise will build on what you put together at the end of the previous chapter. Now, take these steps:

1. Take what you put together and eliminate all *buts* and *howevers*.
2. Consider whether you gave excuses disguised as reasons for having the conversation or if you included true supporting reasons. Be honest with yourself. Re-read the section about excuses if needed.
3. Did you apologize for relaying this message? If so, reflect on why you felt like you needed to insert a sorry. Omit the sorry, and then read what you put together and assess the feelings it evokes. Does it make you feel more confident?

PERSONAL DEVELOPMENT CHALLENGE

Call to mind a boundary that you weren't firm in setting with either a friend, family member, or co-worker. Do you think you might have an opportunity to use the principles of being straightforward, without apologies or excuses, to reinforce this boundary again sometime soon? Tell me about how it goes! Contact me: **conquerstickysituations.com**

The next chapter about being human-centered will tie everything you've learned together and build on what you created in the exercises in the last two chapters. Can you feel the momentum building?

———————————————————

1. If you would like to know more about protected classes, Google Title VII of the Civil Rights Act.
2. I always recommend working with an experienced HR partner to help flesh this out to ensure you do not miss anything and expose yourself to risk.

4

PRONG THREE—HUMAN-CENTERED

The third prong of the five-step process is about making the human connection first, something I call being human-centered. When we come at a situation with a "we can get through this together" mindset, it can open doors we didn't even know were there before. Remembering that we're all humans creates conversations full of options and solutions as opposed to blame and hurtful words. If you use a human-centered approach, you position yourself as a confident and kind leader at work. You'll become someone others can't help but gravitate to—not only at work, but also in life. It's not hard to take this approach once you become aware of it, and this chapter will help you know what to say to keep the conversation human-centered.

BUY IT NOW

My nine-year-old son has been wanting to try snowboarding, so I was hoping to get him a used board so he could try it with little financial investment. Recently, I saw a listing on a local online yard sale page for a kid's snowboard. I reached out to the seller and asked if he was having a good day and whether the board was still available. When he said he still had it, I told him I'd come in the afternoon and pick it up. I made it clear that I understood if it sold before I could get there.

When I picked up the board, I thanked the seller for holding it for me. I told him I appreciated his time and letting me come when I did. As I was about to leave, he said, "I had a lot of others who wanted the snowboard who could have come sooner. I held it for you because you took the time to ask how I was doing and not just send the canned message asking if it was available. That's a rarity these days."

We live in a "Buy It Now" time. We can access so much at the snap of our fingers. Take Amazon, for example. In some cities, they deliver packages within an hour of the order being placed. In many parts of the country, Uber Eats can deliver food whenever and wherever you want. I'm grateful to live in a country where we have these luxuries and this kind of access to almost anything. This option to "Buy It Now" undoubtedly has given us convenience and efficiency. When the choice exists, we tend to opt for the quickest, fastest option (I'm including myself) to enable us to move on to the next thing.

This level of "Buy It Now" and efficiency has a downside, though. We often don't connect when the choice exists for that faster, quicker, and "Buy It Now" option. We're so conditioned to being efficient that we rarely realize opportunities for connection. Maybe we think making a connection takes excessive effort or time and we don't want to deal with it?

I believe this "Buy It Now" culture has taken some of the human-factor from us. I'm not saying we always need to bypass the "Buy It Now" option and sit down and have a long, drawn-out interaction with every person we see. What I'm saying here is if you can connect, I challenge you to not let that opportunity pass every time. Try slowing down a bit to be present in those opportunities for connection. It takes mere seconds to tremendously impact someone else. The smallest things can be more meaningful than you may think—like the small interaction with the snowboard seller I shared here.

CONNECTION QUESTIONS

One good way to slow down and bring more humanity into your interactions is to ask three questions when you have a conversation. You can even think of a handful of questions and use them regularly. They should be thoughtful, sincere, and relevant to the conversation. Try engaging this way when catching up with a friend or when you meet someone new. Taking the time to ask questions shows you're genuinely interested in the other person. You may also learn some really neat things about someone else in the process!

When I'm at a networking event or social gathering, instead of asking the boring question, "So, what do you do?", a favorite question I love to ask is, "What keeps you busy during the day?" I can tell people are intrigued by my asking this question. I like to call these "connection questions."

Here are three of my favorites for when I am networking for business:

- What types of activities interest you?
- How'd you get into your profession?
- What's something interesting about you?

Everyone wants to feel important and valued. Interacting with people in a human-centered way is a simple way to satisfy that desire.

For examples of more connection questions you can try, visit: **conquerstickysituations.com/connectionquestions**

THREE LITTLE WORDS: THE GOLDEN QUESTION

You can accomplish being human-centered in Sticky Conversations with three little words. No, they're not "I love you." At least not literally. At the bottom of it all, that's the basic gist. Love might be a little extreme, but I call these three words the "Golden Question" because they do show the other person you care about them—and that immediately brings the human-factor into the interaction. Are you ready for me to lay them on you?

ARE YOU OKAY?

I can't tell you how many times I delivered workplace management trainings where I saw a light bulb go on in the participants' heads when I shared this tool. It can immediately set a different tone for a feedback or disciplinary meeting. You come at the conversation as someone who wants to first be sure the human behind the issue is okay. This is a great way to find out if there are other factors before you leap right into addressing the issue. This doesn't necessarily mean their answer will change the outcome of the conversation, but it may affect what you say. At work or in life, asking this question may invoke no big reaction ("Yes, I'm fine. Why?") or it may cause tears, frustration, anger, or even silence. Whatever happens, you've caused the air to change. You infused humanity into this interaction with saying these three little words.

Do you need to use this in every conversation? No. Use your judgement. Look at it as a tool you can use when it fits the situation. It's similar to the five steps, where you have a framework, but there is no rule that says you need to use all the steps in every situation.

. . .

The question works in other forms too, as long as the sentiment is the same:

- Are you doing okay?
- How are you?
- How are things?
- I'm worried about you—are you okay?

You may ask - *So I have these words in my sticky employee situation toolbox, but what do I do when they introduce a medical issue or tell me they're getting divorced or tell me something they don't like about me? What if they get angry?*

Don't worry. You'll be okay in any of these scenarios because I'm going to give you an entire chapter of "What If?" tools. You got this!

FRAME YOUR STICKY CONVERSATIONS

Some ways to keep it human-centered when you start a Sticky Conversation is to try beginning with telling the other person you want to get their advice or need their thoughts on a situation. Tell them you're seeking their perspective and value their suggestions. Or, call your Sticky Conversation a "quick talk" or a "brainstorming session." Referring to a conversation as a "mediation" or "conflict/issue resolution" frames the conversation completely differently. Take a minute to step back and consider this before diving into a conversation with angry energy. This doesn't mean you shouldn't be straightforward; it means to remember the human side of the interaction. You *can* have both. Framing it as a conversation where you're open to their perspective from the start allows a different, more positive energy to enter not only your body but the situation.

THREE HUMAN-CENTERED APPROACHES

Just as those few small words from above can work their magic, there are three approaches to Sticky Situations that can also set you up for more productive interactions.

1. Gratitude
2. Empathy
3. Doing Something Worthwhile Today

Before I go into these approaches, I want to be clear about one thing: Taking the human-centered approach doesn't mean being "soft" or beating around the bush. It does mean remembering we're all human and are all part of the human experience. We all have feelings and are impacted positively or negatively by our interactions with others.

GRATITUDE

Gratitude is a core piece of the five steps for handling Sticky Conversations. By definition, it means "the quality of being thankful; readiness to show appreciation for and to return kindness."[1] I will admit, I'm kind of obsessed with gratitude. There's incredible power in thankfulness and expressing gratitude. When you're grateful and appreciative of your life and those around you, you may notice things work more smoothly. You get through your day with more ease. Whether we notice or not, we're more joyful and affect the people who surround us more positively when we're in a state of gratitude. If you believe in the universe and universal intelligence, then you know the universe loves when we fill our hearts with gratitude. When the universe is happy with you, your life can transform. The universe notices when you exude gratefulness and will want to give you more things you can be thankful for.

My parents are two of the nicest people you'll ever meet. They are always wanting to know how they can help my sister and me, and those around them. My dad, Bob, has very little hair and a tin of Altoids at the ready at any moment. My kids and I fondly call him "Pep," after his Canadian dad, "Pépère," which means grandfather in French. Pep is grateful for everything in life and believes everyone has good intentions. Pep is the epitome of the "glass half full" mentality. On cloudy days, which are common on the East Coast where I grew up, he cheerily says, "The sun is gonna win out! You watch!"

I skied a lot growing up. On Saturday mornings, my dad and I drove to McDonalds to get Egg McMuffin sandwiches on our way to Wachusett Mountain for me to take part in the junior ski patrol. Once we were settled with our sandwiches, in his Boston accent, my dad would ask me "So, Jill, what are you grateful fahhh?" I'd answer with what I was grateful for, and my dad would follow. I am so fortunate to have been exposed to gratefulness from a young age. I was one lucky kid to have had Mary and Bob as parents and the opportunity to learn from them.

To be proficient with practicing gratitude, you must take the time to practice daily. In my life, I set an intention and conscious choice to build gratitude into every day. I make sure to always express my gratitude in emails I write for work or personally. I often tell my friends I'm grateful for their friendship for specific reasons. I told a friend the other day I appreciate our conversations and love her insights on what we talk about. I think it took her off guard, but I could tell it made her feel fantastic. Expressing gratitude is important—and if you can be super specific about exactly what you're grateful about, you magnify its power.

A habit I've kept into adulthood, thanks to Pep, is to say out loud what I'm grateful for. I do this while walking my dog or during my morning routine. You can do it any time that works for you. A lot of people work this into their morning drive to work, for example. Try saying three things you're grateful for at the moment. Expressing your gratitude practice out loud reinforces the pathway for gratefulness in your brain. If you have a morning routine (I give you one at the end of this book!), try incorporating your gratitude practice then. Some days I repeat what I'm thankful for from the day before. Other mornings, I list new reasons to be grateful. There are no rules; gratitude has no one right way. Gratitude is how I reflect on life, what's going on around me and with those I love.

Learning to incorporate more gratitude into your life is like working a muscle. When you start, it's new and awkward, and you need to remind yourself to keep doing it. This is because it's not yet a habit. As you work your "gratitude muscle" more often, it will become more habitual and come more naturally. Not only will it require less effort, but it will also make you stronger, like you get when you make working out a habit.

There are so many ways to practice gratitude. It's about the mindset it creates, not the specifics of your approach. Some popular ways to practice gratitude are:

- Gratitude journals (can be a simple blank notebook or a designated gratitude journal)
- Shout what you're grateful for out into the world.
- Use a planner, like the Panda Planner, which has a section for listing three things you're grateful for each day.

The benefits of gratitude at work and in our personal lives are endless. Gratitude can increase our productivity, overall personal sense of well-being and happiness, and can even lower anxiety and worry. Expressing gratitude literally lowers the stress hormone cortisol in our bodies. When I'm intentional about focusing on gratitude, I physically feel less stress through my neck and shoulders. Dopamine, a hormone responsible for allowing us to feel pleasure, also increases when we express gratitude and think grateful thoughts. Both at work and in our personal lives, we are more likely to be more productive if we're feeling good about our work and motivated to keep doing it. Feeling good enables us to form more powerful relationships with those around us. We radiate happiness and joy. At work, when we have better relationships, not only are we more productive but we're also more creative because we're working in harmony with those around us and communicate more effectively.

All this said, sometimes focusing on gratitude is hard, so hard. When I'm in a rough spot, sometimes it takes so much effort that I don't want to focus on the positive and be grateful. What to do in those self-pity times? Double-down on gratitude! Trust me. These are the times to dig deep. Don't give up and throw away all the gratitude work you've done because you're in a rough patch. Challenge yourself to shift your focus from the things that are setting you back to the things that are going right and continue to propel you forward. Start by finding just one thing that's going right, even if it's tough. If you get one, you'll probably find more. I've had this experience, and I've seen the effect coming back to gratitude has had on me. Gratitude resets me mentally—that's my motivation to always return to it. It puts me in a better place where I can be sound in my decision-making. This improved mental space enables me to be laser-focused on the right priorities each day.

Gratitude is a fantastic conduit for inserting positive energy into life and work. If you adopt a habit of gratefulness, research supports that you'll build better relationships and be more productive, especially at work. I encourage you to think about gratefulness in the workplace not as an option but as a must, as long as it's sincere. Your employees will see right through you if you're fake about expressing gratitude.

The good news is that starting a gratitude practice need not be big and monumental—the small things are the big things. And, if you're getting ready to have a Sticky Conversation, here are three ways to open with gratitude, which will start the conversation off on the right foot:

- Thank you for taking a few minutes to meet with me.
- I appreciate you taking time out of your busy day to talk with me.
- I know you're busy and I very much appreciate you taking the time to discuss this with me.

I also recommend closing with gratitude.

- This must have been hard for you to come talk to me about this. I appreciate the courage it took.
- Thank you for hearing me out and listening to my concerns.
- I appreciate your openness to having this discussion. Thanks again.

There is always a place for gratitude at work and in life. Infuse the wonderful energy that comes with being grateful into all you do, and you *will* see results.

EXAMPLES: GRATITUDE AT WORK

There are many opportunities to incorporate gratitude at work whether you're expressing it to others or feeling it internally. Saying a sincere "thank you" is one of the most obvious ways to show your gratitude at work. Be careful not to discount this; it may be one of the simplest ways to express gratitude—but it's also one of the most effective. When you say "thank you," be specific and sincere. Do it often. Form a habit.

When it comes to experiencing gratitude, I have a simple trick you can try. Put a few paper clips in one pocket in the morning. Consider each of the clips a way to express gratitude during the day. Each time you experience gratitude, move one clip to the other pocket. Try to do this each work day. Before you know it, you won't need the clips because you will have developed a habit of gratefulness at work. And there are plenty of other ways you can easily incorporate gratitude at work in the morning, during meetings, and even during terminations.

GRATITUDE IN THE MORNING

Coffee drinkers, consider this morning gratitude routine like your morning coffee. It's not an option—it's a necessity!

Take it one step further and see a gratitude practice as your "morning jolt" at work, like the caffeine in your coffee. If you're a manager of a department, you can express gratitude when you see your team in the morning. "Good morning! Thanks for being here!" Or, try telling someone you pass in the office, "It's nice to see you! Seeing you here this morning brightened my day." Sure, they have to be there at work to get paid, but still, there's no reason you shouldn't express gratitude for seeing them. It may feel strange initially, but, remember, showing gratitude will become part of who you are as your brain is trained to find opportunities for gratefulness everywhere around you.

Opportunities to express gratefulness are everywhere in life. They're easy to find if you train your mind to be aware and open to them.

GRATITUDE DURING MEETINGS

For those of you who manage employees, I challenge you to think of one thing each person on your team did the day or week before that you can call out in a daily stand-up or staff meeting. When being grateful to your team, don't forget that being specific about what you're grateful for comes across as more sincere.

Work Meeting Gratitude Bonus Trick: If you call out work well done for someone verbally in a meeting, follow it with a super quick email to reiterate what the praise was. They hear it twice and you both get twice the "gratefulness jolt." A win-win!

YES, EVEN GRATITUDE DURING TERMINATIONS!

Let's talk about one of the stickiest of all Sticky Situations—employee terminations. Not fun for anyone. Those getting fired likely feel sadness and despair, among other emotions. You can't express gratitude or thank them for a job well done, obviously, since they're getting fired. You can express gratitude, though, for them having worked at the company. The reality is they performed work, it may not have been the best work, but they still worked. Even though they performed poorly or made one too many mistakes, we can still treat them with dignity on their way out. At least honor this for them. It improves the experience for the departing employee. Heck, it may even protect your company from poor reviews.

EXAMPLES: *HOW TO EXPRESS GRATITUDE DURING AN EMPLOYEE TERMINATION*

- Thanks for the work you did with the company. We wish you the best.
- We appreciate the work you did for us. We're sorry your employment has to end this way.
- Thanks for the efforts you gave to try and resolve your performance issues. The decision was difficult for us. We wish you the best.

Resentful feelings by the manager can accompany an involuntary termination. Often managers arrive to a termination frustrated because things haven't been going right for a long period. For this exact reason, gratitude is often left out because the person giving the news is so focused on what went wrong and their emotions around it. I encourage intentionality about putting those feelings of resentment or frustration aside during a termination.

I hope you see how inserting gratitude doesn't mean you need to invest a lot of extra energy or time. In fact, inserting a gratitude practice into your daily life can be done almost effortlessly, if you learn techniques and make it a habit.

EMPATHY

Empathy is the ability to put yourself in someone else's shoes and relate personally to what they're feeling.

Sympathy is when you feel sorrow or pity for someone, and is commonly referred to as feeling bad for someone.

Let's say you recently heard bad news from a good friend. Maybe a parent has cancer, or she found out she's infertile. You frantically search for the right words to say to show you care and want to help, but nothing comes to mind. You panic and freeze, not sure what to do. Ever been in a similar situation? I know I have, many times. Until I studied empathy more and got a true understanding of what it is, I felt inept to respond in these situations.

It is so hard to know what to say in a situation calling for empathy. Often, our well-meaning responses backfire and we end up making someone who's already in a tough place of hurting feel worse. Like many things, developing empathy is a skill you must work on.

There is a misconception about empathy. Some think you need to like or care about the person you're feeling empathetic toward. The reality is we won't like everyone we meet. We still should learn empathy and how to show it toward others whether we like them or not. Empathy is a great tool for building relationships—especially when used with people you don't like.

Many people confuse empathy and sympathy. When you talk about empathy, people who don't understand the difference may cut you off and groan and then tell you they're not "a touchy-feely kind of person." They ask, "Do I have to be empathetic in the workplace?"

Many situations call for empathy, yet we automatically respond with sympathy. We feel bad for the person going through something difficult and say, "I feel bad for you." Attempting to understand their situation fully and truly putting ourselves in their position to feel their pain and struggles is much tougher to do. Empathy is taking on their pain and feeling what it's like. When we outline the difference, it seems obvious which builds a relationship with someone. Brené Brown says it so well, "Empathy fuels connection; sympathy drives disconnection."[2]

Before starting a Sticky Conversation, pause and think about how you'd feel if the message was being delivered to you. This is being empathetic to the person who's hearing the news from you. How would you like it relayed to you? This is a great starting place to ensure you insert the human factor through empathy in these conversations.

It doesn't matter what generation you're in. Everyone wants others to understand the pain they're going through or how they feel. I challenge you to practice empathy in your everyday life by trying to empathize when you're on the road and someone is driving aggressively. Perhaps it is not them, but something they're going through that's making them act this way. Calling on empathy gives us an opportunity to see the situation through a new lens.

EXAMPLE: EMPATHY IN ACTION

Let's take an employee who is always having trouble getting to work on time. We'll call her Kathy. More than half the time, she would say she would be into the office late, then call to say she wouldn't make it in after all. In this scenario, let's also say that she has been employed for less than six months when she started calling out. The reasons she gave for the absences were that her kids were sick or that she did not have daycare. Her manager was at wits' end with the tardiness and absences. The manager struggled with how to address it since the employee would get emotional whenever the topic came up saying that she was a single parent with young kids. In these situations, the easy thing to do would be to disregard the employee's personal situation and discipline as per the company policy. Instead, it is worth the time to pause, step back from the situation, and look at it through an empathetic lens. Let's say the manager took the empathetic approach and called the employee to their office to discuss the issue.

Manager: Hi, Kathy. How are things going?

Kathy: (Tearing up immediately.) Not good. I know everyone is annoyed at me for missing so much work and for being late a lot. No one understands where I'm coming from! I'm a single parent, and it's so hard because I have no one to rely on except myself when my kids are sick. (She cries.)

Manager: (Pauses before speaking to ensure she completed her thought. Hands her some tissues.) It must be hard to be a single parent with all the expectations at work, especially when the learning curve at a new job is hard. When things come up in our personal lives, it's difficult to make it all work.

Kathy: I have no relatives living nearby which makes it even harder to manage.

Manager: It is hard not to have a support system, especially when you have kids. (Pause. Listen. Let her talk until the conversation lulls. Then transition to discussing the performance issues and the impact on the team.) The team needs you to be in the office during the work day. When you're not here, your tasks fall on someone else's shoulders. They don't mind helping once in a while. Covering too much causes a drop in morale and team frustration. For this reason, it is important that we are having this conversation. We want to accommodate your needs as best we can as well as balance the needs of the team.

As you saw in this example, being empathetic is attempting to imagine what it would be like to be in that person's situation and what the experience is like for them *first* before jumping into addressing issues. Let's say this was a real situation and that Kathy was receptive to the feedback. (This is not unrealistic; I have seen this happen in my experience with similar situations.) Employees often respond by taking the initiative to brainstorm ways they can fix their performance issues when they feel like they were heard and that others understand what they are going through. This leads to them feeling more empowered to find solutions. In my experience, when I approached Sticky Situations at work with empathy, employees often came back to my office later and thanked me for taking the time to hear where they were coming from.

Kathy: Thanks for understanding my situation. It means a lot that you let me vent about things. I know my being late and absent from work is an issue that affects the whole team. I am going to ask a friend if she can help me with childcare, and maybe I can help her when I am off work. I know I need to get to work or it's going to affect my job.

Whether in life or at work, when we tap into empathy and attempt to see where the other person is coming from before addressing issues, it goes a long way. Situations don't always end up how we hope they will, but nine times out of ten, things are smoother when we step back and approach Sticky Situations with empathy first.

The third way to be more human-centered is about doing something small but worthwhile today . . . and every day.

DO SOMETHING WORTHWHILE TODAY

Some people ask why I make sure I do something worthwhile every day. I ask them back, Why not? We humans seek meaning and purpose in our lives. The problem is that the busyness of life impedes us from feeling like we can do something worthwhile each day and find this meaning. Making money, working demanding jobs, kids, commitments, hobbies—all the stuff that clutters our lives leaves no space for anything else. We can easily get caught up in "finding our true calling" and "making a difference." We forget to take small worthwhile actions daily and in the present moment. It's easy to miss the opportunities around us to make a difference and insert a little humanness. I encourage you to pause and look at opportunities to do something, no matter how small, that is worthwhile today.

Where to start? Try starting with your current environment. Use where you are or where you'll go today as starting places to do something worthwhile.

- Do something special for yourself—yes, *yourself!* We need to care for ourselves before we can care for anyone else.
- Stop what you're doing (I'll even let you put down this book!) and hug your partner.
- Hug your kid—don't let go until they do.
- Buy someone a donut for no reason.
- At the grocery store, smile at people as you pass them in the aisles. You may startle people, but you'll probably draw many return smiles from people you try this on. Or

if you're brave and want to take it to the next level, I challenge you to say "Hello!" along with your smile. Now you'll really startle people. I do this and always leave the store with that smile still in place.

- Call a children's hospital near you and see if they need people to hold newborns in the NICU.
- Ask if you can volunteer in your kid's class or at a local library reading books to the kids, or devote 15 minutes each day to read to your child. Be energetic, use silly voices, be the most fun version of yourself for the short time to read the book. Your kids will remember this.
- Offer to buy the grocery store cashier and bagger a candy bar or a bottled beverage as they ring your groceries. They're ensuring your eggs don't smash and your canned beans don't squish your Ruffles; they deserve a thank you. I do this often and am graciously received with an "Oh my gosh, this is the nicest thing anyone has ever done for me!"
- I often see people who backtrack to get a bag when their dog takes a number two. If you have a bag, pick it up for them.
- Send money to your favorite charity—even a few dollars matter.
- Next time you're grocery shopping, snag an extra bag of dog or cat food and some treats and drop them at the local animal shelter. While you're there, ask if you can take the dog who's been at the shelter the longest for a quick stroll.
- Send a quick text or email to someone and tell them specifically how much you value them and their friendship. Example: "I wanted to tell you I value you and your friendship. When you called the other day to ask how my project at work was going, it meant a lot to me. Thank you again for bringing brightness to my otherwise stressful day." How often has a little ray-of-

sunshine text like this popped onto your phone?
Imagine what feelings it would evoke to be received.

- Send a paper thank you or "thinking of you" card to someone. Who doesn't love opening an actual paper letter in the mail?
- Give a buck or two to someone on the street. If you're worrying about whether they'll spend the money in useful or self-destructive ways, let that go.
- Buy a receptionist a coffee and a donut. (Can you tell I'm a big fan of donuts?)
- Surprise the person behind you at Starbucks by buying them their coffee. (This is one of my favorites.)
- Buy a copy of this book for someone who is struggling with a Sticky Situation.

The seemingly little things are often the big things. Brake for a minute and ask yourself, What small, worthwhile action can I take today?

THREE "HUMAN-CENTERED" NUGGETS

- MYTH: Being human-centered takes a lot of extra time; FACT: Being human-centered takes little or no extra time.
- Two easy ways to incorporate the human-factor into your communications: Gratitude and Empathy
- Try opening a Sticky Conversation with the Golden Question, "Are you okay?" or "How are things?"

RECAP

In this chapter, you learned what it means to be human-centered at work and in life, and how it applies to handling Sticky Situations. I showed you how being human-centered need not take a lot of time or extra energy. In the next "What If?" chapter, I address scenarios where unexpected things come up, some of which are from my personal experience. These will help you when handling your next Sticky Situation.

YOU GOT THIS! LET'S PRACTICE . . .

To practice being more human-centered, we'll build off the exercises you did in the last two chapters. Reviewing what you put together so far:

1. Did you thank the person for having the conversation either at the beginning or end or in both places?
2. Are there places in this scripted conversation where you could have applied a more human-centered approach? Did you make sure it's clear that you care about the other person/that you value them or that their work is valuable to the team if it's a work example?
3. Can you start the conversation by asking if the person is okay? Review the options for this type of opening if needed.
4. If appropriate to the situation, did you express empathy? What words did you use? Were you truly showing empathy or was it sympathy?

PERSONAL DEVELOPMENT CHALLENGE

List below what small worthwhile thing you will do today, tomorrow, and the next day—three things. Reference the list I provided in this chapter or create your own. The idea is to get you started by writing these things down and committing to them. Keep writing them down each day until it becomes a habit. Starting a "Worthwhile Today" notebook is a great way to ensure this is a priority. Tell me about what you did that was worthwhile today!

Contact me: **conquerstickysituations.com**

1.

2.

3.

You've done the preparation, and now you're ready! Review what you put together a few times to make sure you're clear on what you need to say. And then . . . drum roll, please . . . conquer the Sticky Conversation!

---

1. "Gratitude," Lexico, https://www.lexico.com/en/definition/gratitude.
2. "Brené Brown on Empathy," RSA short, Dec. 10, 2013, video, 2:53, https://www.youtube.com/watch?v=1Evwgu369Jw.

5

WHAT IF?

B efore we hop to the examples, I'm including one more tool to handle Sticky Conversations, and it's one of my favorites. When I guide my clients through a Sticky Situation, I always talk about what I call "What if?" scenarios. We can form what we think is a solid plan to handle a Sticky Situation, but if unexpected things come up, our plan can go sideways . . . fast. When we don't plan for the "What if?" scenarios, we can quickly lose control and end up frustrated—right back where we started, or in a worse place. While I won't be able to capture all "What if?" scenarios here, I'll share a few common ones from my experience. These types of scenarios also apply to helping you navigate unexpected responses if you ask the "Are you okay?" question at the beginning of a Sticky Conversation.

The "What if?" scenarios can generally all fall into one of three categories: Emotions, Hostile Response, and Additional or Unexpected Information.

EMOTIONS

I would be remiss if I didn't acknowledge emotions as they relate to Sticky Situations. These conversations often elicit emotions because the message is hard to hear. Emotions are also often triggered when there is an underlying issue, which falls under example number three, "Additional or Unexpected Information."

Emotions are natural, especially because these are not your everyday situations—they're the stickiest situations! Emotions can bubble up suddenly in the person starting the conversation or the person receiving the message. I'm an advocate of always being prepared. Regardless of whether you think there will be emotions on either side of the conversation, keep some tissues handy.

The goal with handling a Sticky Situation is to not make it personal. You should ensure the person you're having the conversation with doesn't feel belittled or embarrassed. Despite your best efforts, this can happen unintentionally, especially in Sticky Situations that address hygiene or inappropriate clothing. (You'll find sample scripts in chapter 7, "Tying It All Together.") When emotions surface, pause for a minute and offer tissues. This is where the human factor comes in. Try not to charge ahead immediately with what you planned to say. There will be time for this soon enough.

Give the person a minute or two, or whatever is appropriate for the situation and how much emotion they're showing, and then carry on with what you planned to say. What you don't want to do is bag the entire conversation because you encountered emotions and you feel awkward. Sticky Situations *are* awkward; there's no way around it. One way to prepare is to go into the conversation expecting emotions and understanding they're natural, as we are all human beings.

Being silent for a minute and giving respect to the emotions is one tool. Another is acknowledging the emotions with a simple sentence, such as, "I know this is hard to hear. It's normal to feel emotional."

It's a good idea to factor in time for the possibility of emotions to surface. Setting too short of a time frame for a Sticky Conversation then having emotions come up can add stress. You've had enough stress and/or worry about the situation in the first place, so be smart about planning the needed time.

HOSTILE RESPONSE

By hostile response, I am referring to either a physically hostile action or a verbal attack. The best way to prepare for this is to take precautions and put measures in place before the conversation.

At work, this may look like having someone standing by outside the room where you're having the tough conversation. Placing them there is a precaution if the employee angers suddenly or gets hostile and you need support. If there's a high level of concern, this preparation may involve alerting the building security and/or giving a heads-up to local law enforcement about a predicted or potential outcome.

For sticky employee terminations, I recommend erring on the side of caution and putting at least one of the aforementioned back-up/support options in place. In my experience, clients thanked me every time I recommended considering these "What if?" scenarios and said they never would have considered these things. I witnessed otherwise mellow and quiet employees become outraged when getting fired, storm back to their desk where others are sitting, and begin yelling at the top of their lungs about what a rotten workplace it is. It can get messy fast.

Please listen when I recommend taking this into serious consideration.

In non-work life situations, if you worry about a hostile reaction to what you say, a similar but slightly different approach applies. Consider having someone who can be trusted nearby as support. Be sure this is someone who you know can be respectful of the situation and keep it confidential. They can sit somewhere nearby, hardly noticeable, but where they can hear if things escalate.

At work or in life, you should do your best to assess and gauge the likelihood of a hostile response. Plan accordingly in advance and use good judgement with preparation.[1]

ADDITIONAL OR UNEXPECTED INFORMATION

> *The work examples in this section are not meant to be a deep-dive into HR. The goal is to give you tools to start you off on the right foot when the unexpected happens. It is always recommended to seek professional legal or HR guidance if you are unsure how to proceed.*

This "What if?" scenario refers to information that comes up in the conversation, with or without emotions, that you didn't know prior. A few topics that may come up as additional or unexpected information are:

- Medical condition
- Divorce
- Illness of a family member

When these things pop up, the best thing you can do is pause the conversation, either momentarily or until a later date. I caution you with immediately charging ahead with your planned script. Pausing gives you a minute to digest what they shared and assess next steps. It is still important to address the issue, just with adjusted timing depending on the issue.

This may look like a friend telling you they are having financial troubles after you tell them the issue with them borrowing money from you. At work, it may be when you are addressing a performance issue and the employee says the reason for the issue is due to a medical condition, or that they are getting divorced. In both cases, you were not aware of this until this moment. You don't need to take back the feedback, but you may not want to proceed right away. Pause. Recall what you learned about empathy in chapter 4. Don't pretend to know what they're going through. Express how you would feel if you were in their shoes. (Even if you have experienced something similar, that does not mean your experience is the same as theirs.) Give them space to talk for a few minutes if they choose. Listen and do not interrupt. (I don't recommend probing about the situation— focus on empathy instead.) Ask them if there is something you can do to provide support.

Consider asking yourself these questions when determining how to care about the person as a human first before addressing the issues:

- Do you know of any local or online resources to which you can direct them?
- Have you had a similar experience and can perhaps offer things that helped you? (It is important to remember that everyone's experience is different. Share your experience, if applicable to the situation, but don't push them to do what you did.)
- Could you offer that they leave work early that day as a kind gesture? (Perhaps tell them you will regroup the next morning.)

- Can you give them a day or two off work to see their doctor or to meet with a lawyer, or something else their work schedule may have previously not allowed for?
- Can you provide them additional benefits plan information or offer to connect them directly with a plan representative to answer any of their medical questions about their condition?
- Does your company offer an Employee Assistance Program (often referred to as an EAP) to which you can direct them for various support options?

It can never hurt to prepare for a "What if?" scenario when you're planning your Sticky Conversation. Use the exercises at the end of this chapter as a guide to outline the "what ifs" for your particular situation. This process is well worth your time, as it will help position you for success if the unplanned happens.

THREE "WHAT IF?" NUGGETS

- Having a "What if?" plan in place prepares you for when the unexpected happens.
- Hostile situations are often not expected, so it is crucial to put measures in place just in case, especially in termination situations.
- Having these "What if?" tools handy will help you resolve an issue instead of having to put it off and address later, prolonging the issue.

RECAP

In this chapter, I outlined some common "What if?" scenarios when you're addressing Sticky Situations. I also helped you with what to do if a situation catches you off guard and you suddenly find yourself in a Sticky Conversation. Keeping these scenarios in mind while applying the five-step formula and the three-pronged simple, straightforward, and human-centered approach will help ensure a "What if?" scenario won't throw you off track if it happens. Taking the time to think through all "What if?" scenarios and preparing will best set you up for success in handling Sticky Situations.

YOU GOT THIS! LET'S PRACTICE . . .

Review what you put together in the exercises for your script to handle a Sticky Situation.

1. Is there a "What if?" scenario from this chapter which may apply to your specific Sticky Situation?
2. If you answered no to #1 above, what are some other "What if?" scenarios you can think of that may happen?
3. Think of a couple ways you will handle it if those "What if?" scenarios happen. Refer to the questions in this chapter for ways you could show you care before proceeding with the conversation.

PERSONAL DEVELOPMENT CHALLENGE

Uncertainty in not knowing how a Sticky Situation will end can be very unsettling. I'm writing this during the COVID-19 pandemic—talk about uncertain times! I challenge you to allow yourself to feel the uncertainty in any given situation. Give yourself the space to sit with that feeling. When we allow ourselves to accept when a situation feels uncertain, it's only then that we can start the process of moving through it. We can then sift through it in a calm, rational manner and clearly outline our plan. Below, write something that feels uncertain in your life right now. It may be a Sticky Situation in your work or personal life, or in the world in general, like the pandemic. Write down three things that are uncertain.

Example: My job and company's viability during the pandemic.

1.
2.
3.

Write three things that are *not* uncertain and are in your control related to this situation.

Example: My resume—I can set aside time to ensure it is updated in case I were to lose my job so I am ready to search for another.

1.
2.
3.

If you need to, partner with someone who may have the same uncertainty and put your heads together on coming up with these lists. When I do this exercise, I feel a comforting sense of control.

1.
2.
3.

I want to hear about all the ways you're strong, resilient, and resourceful which came through in the above exercise. Contact me: **conquerstickysituations.com**

---

1. Since all employment terminations are unique, I recommend seeking legal or HR consultant advice. This helps ensure you have the right documentation in place and mitigates risk.

6

BONUS "WHAT IF?" TOOLS

As a special treat, I'm sharing two bonus "What if?" tools with you. I'm fond of the first because it's applicable to so many situations, and I'm fond of the second for the exact opposite reason. It helps you know how to handle situations that, despite trying to expect the unexpected, you still haven't anticipated.

THE POWERFUL PAUSE

The Powerful Pause is a well-loved tool of mine because it's incredibly effective, yet so simple, and can be applied to a wide variety of situations.

Do you ever end a conversation at work or with a friend and later wish you'd listened better or asked more thoughtful questions? If you're a high energy person like me, you may have to constantly remind yourself to slow down and pause more often. Remember what Ferris Bueller told us? Life moves pretty fast; if you don't slow down, you could miss it. We're so quick to press the "Buy It Now" button. We want everything immediately, including solutions and answers to all our questions.

Pausing for even a few seconds can be transformative in our lives and the way we interact with others—at work, when conflict arises, and when we feel pushed to decide on the spot. Pausing a conversation and revisiting it later is a super simple but hugely effective tool. We're all human. Sometimes we cannot muster compassion or the right words in a meeting. This is when you should take advantage of the Powerful Pause. Stop the conversation. Revisit later, after you've had time to think through next steps. It will benefit not only you but the person you're having the conversation with.

In HR leadership roles, sometimes there is an expectation to have an answer or a workable solution to any issue presented, whether small or complex. Even armed with my years of experience and skills, I still didn't always know the best course of action in the moment. When I dug into the issue and thought through the request, after pausing the conversation, and revisiting at a later time, I was able to come up with a solution.

The overarching blueprint for using this tactic is to thank the person for bringing this issue/idea/question to your attention. Paraphrase what they're asking/requesting back to them. Then let them know you'd like to take some time to review the facts to guide them most appropriately, and let them know you'll respond within 24 hours.

Suggest a Powerful Pause if you find yourself witnessing a heated dispute between friends, family members, co-workers, or perhaps between employees you manage. Suggest to those involved that they should consider pausing the conversation and stepping away to regroup before it escalates. Share with them techniques you learned in this book. You are in a great spot to empower them to revisit the Sticky Situation with a more level head and a fresh approach.

EXAMPLES: USING THE POWERFUL PAUSE

Let's say you're a manager and you need to bring two of your employees together who you know are having a disagreement. The issue has been going on for over a month and needs to be resolved.

Here's what the conversation may look like:

> You: "I brought us together with the hopes of resolving the issue at hand. It was brought to my attention that this issue is causing a big disruption in your department. It's important we get the issues on the table and proactively find solutions." (You then ask one of the parties to describe, from their point of view, what is going on.)

> Person A starts by describing what she sees as the primary issues, but quickly goes off track and begins to bring up irrelevant details and some surprising, previously unknown, details. The dialogue quickly moves to Person A accusing Person B of wrongdoing.

> Person B jumps in, "No, that's not true at all! This isn't what happened!" Person B goes on to dispute what was said, introduce new issues from their point of view, and other things you were unaware of.

> You assess the fact that there is a lot of new information. You need time to process all this. Now is the time to employ the Powerful Pause.

> You: "I'm going to interject here and ask you both to pause the conversation. I see there are many issues, some of which I just heard about today. We'll need to revisit this issue at a later time once I have a bit of time to reflect on what was said. This time may be good to give

you both the opportunity to reflect on what was brought up as well. Thanks for your time today. I'll contact you each within 24 hours about next steps."

Another great time for the Powerful Pause is when an issue pops up very unexpectedly. For example, your boss comes to you and accuses you of not getting along well with a co-worker or has an issue with the way you completed a project. We sometimes respond too quickly, often resulting in a defensive response. In this situation, you can say, "Thanks for the feedback." This shows you were listening to the feedback. When you resist lashing out with a quick response or being defensive and reactive, it shows professionalism. Pause. Powerful, right? Next, calmly tell them you'd like to take a bit of time to reflect on the conversation and finish it later. This approach allows you to determine if there is truth to the assertion in a calm, nonreactive setting. Even if you determine the feedback was unfounded, you're better off for not having reacted at the moment and to have paused the conversation. You gave yourself the gift of being able to collect your thoughts and the time to be able to step away. You will now be in a better spot to craft a simple and clear response for when you reconnect with your manager on the issue.

When I'm consulting with clients, they often ask me "What if?" questions, such as:

- What if, after I relay feedback, they tell me what I shared with them is wrong?
- What if they tell me something I didn't know, and it changes the direction of the conversation?
- What if they lash out at me verbally?

These are the perfect scenarios to activate the Powerful Pause to buy yourself time to formulate your thoughts. The Powerful

Pause has wonderful applications in our everyday lives too. You can use it if you find yourself unsure how to respond in a tough conversation with a spouse, good friend, or relative. The Powerful Pause is especially valuable if someone verbally attacks you. It will keep you from responding quickly and saying something you will regret. Give yourself a timeline to calm down and plan sensible thoughts about the issue before responding.

As a job applicant, using the Powerful Pause can be a good idea before you answer an interview question to ensure your response is as thoughtful as possible. Years back, I did some career coaching, and this is one tool I always gave job seekers when I coached them. Pause when you don't know how to respond to an interview question. It's much better than quickly answering with a thoughtless response that could even cost you the interview. I've conducted hundreds of interviews, and candidates who paused before answering questions always impressed me. It shows confidence and shows they don't want to rush to answer. They want what comes out of their mouth to be thoughtful and meaningful. They want to ensure they can accurately answer the actual interview question.

In everyday conversations, wouldn't you want people to know you as someone who thinks before speaking? When people talk about you, would you like to be described as thoughtful and insightful? If you pause after another person has finished speaking, you're much less likely to interrupt them. Glorious things happen when you incorporate the Powerful Pause into your "life toolbox." I hope you find reassurance in always knowing you have this tool in your back pocket at work and in your personal life.

EXPECT THE UNEXPECTED

A second bonus "What if?" scenario I'd like to share is what to do if a Sticky Situation catches you off guard. Imagine that you're approached by someone needing to address an issue with you, or perhaps you're cornered and asked for a response about something.

What a fine mess this is! There you are—unprepared and flustered. You know the five-step process, but had no chance to prepare and did *not* expect this confrontation. Don't worry, there are tools that you can rely on to prepare you for the unexpected.

I understand the reality of life and that situations come up that we can't plan for. Sometimes we don't have adequate time to prepare in advance for a Sticky Conversation. Perhaps someone pulls us aside at work and confronts us on a work task, or we're at a social gathering and a friend or relative starts accusing us of something. My goal is that you've studied and practiced the steps and ingrained them in your mind, so you can easily tap into them when you suddenly find yourself in the Sticky Situation! That said, I still want to provide you some tools—Breathe, Safety Scripts, and Step Back or Walk Away—to call on if you find yourself blindsided by a Sticky Situation.

BREATHE

Just breathe! When confronted with something suddenly, one of the best tools is . . . to breathe! Too often, we forget this super simple tool, which can help us in our lives and work situations. Take a deep breath immediately once you realize what's happening. Say to yourself in your head, "Uh oh, I'm in a Sticky Situation right now!" and have that trigger you to take a big deep breath. Say nothing right away. There is science behind this. When you breathe deeply, it sends a message to your brain to calm down and relax. The brain then sends this same message to your body which results in you feeling less agitated and able to think clearly.

Tap into the Powerful Pause tool from earlier in this chapter as you breathe.

SAFETY SCRIPTS

I have a few short scripts, some of which are one-liners, that I'll share with you to use when you suddenly find yourself confronted or in the middle of a Sticky Conversation. I call these "Safety Scripts."

Memorize one or two, or a combination, that feel most natural to you. These are universal for work and life. I recommend breathing before saying any of these. It makes you sound calmer and less flustered. One of my favorites which may ring a bell is "Thank you for the feedback." It's easy to remember and works in a wide variety of situations. It also sounds extremely professional if you receive hard feedback at work but manage to respond with gratitude. Talk about taking the high road!

EXAMPLES: SAFETY SCRIPTS

- I feel taken aback by what you told me. I'd like a minute to process and revisit later.
- I hear what you're saying (said). I am choosing not to respond to this right now. I'd like to revisit this conversation once I've composed my thoughts.
- Thanks for bringing this to my attention. I'm sure it was hard for you to say something.
- This is hard for me to hear, but I'm glad you said something. (A "but" is okay here because you're saying something and then use the word "but" to show that you see two sides of the situation.)

STEP BACK OR WALK AWAY

When confronted, you may feel you need to remove yourself from the situation. This may come in the form of backing up a step or two, or walking away to regain composure. If you know your personality and your blood boils when confronted, say nothing and walk away. You're human and it's normal to get flustered in these moments. We need to know ourselves enough to assess whether we can call upon a calming tool or a script to get us through, or if we're simply better off to walk away. Sometimes it's best to revisit the conversation later. This way, we buy time to digest what we heard and prepare our response.

Stepping back is a body language cue that you were literally and figuratively taken aback by what was said. Your action relays that you're feeling uncomfortable and says a lot without words. From there, you can choose to say something or proceed to walk away.

Walking away is setting a boundary. You will not accept the way the person approached you at that moment. The boundary says that you won't let someone force you to have a conversation when it doesn't feel right for you. I'll preface this by saying that, at work, when your boss calls a sudden meeting to review your performance, you don't always have the luxury of walking away. You can use this tool if you're in a meeting and are taken aback by something said to you. You can calmly get up and leave the room for fear of responding in a way you may regret. From an HR perspective, I would much rather see this than have an altercation ensue.

While walking away is a great tool, I encourage you to have one line you can say before you walk away. Sometimes walking away silently can have more of a negative effect than intended and upset others. That said, walking away is still better than spouting off something you will regret later if you can't remain calm.

EXAMPLES: *ONE LINERS TO OFFER BEFORE WALKING AWAY*

1. I can't have this conversation right now.
2. I need a minute. I'll connect with you a little later.
3. Excuse me.

You will see there are no apologies in there for walking away. This isn't something you need to apologize for. State what you're doing, that's it. You also don't need an apology when you revisit the conversation at a later time.

THREE BONUS "WHAT IF?" NUGGETS

- Even though you didn't have a chance to prepare for the Sticky Conversation in advance, you now have tools to handle it when it blindsides you.
- The Powerful Pause is an incredible tool that helps you focus and regroup in tough situations.
- Even when surprised, you *will* be okay! Remember to breathe, have a "one-liner" memorized and ready, and you can always walk away.

RECAP

There you have it. Two bonus "What if?" tools—the Powerful Pause and the Expect the Unexpected toolbox. Keeping these responses in mind will help you to not go off track when the unexpected strikes.

YOU GOT THIS! LET'S PRACTICE . . .

Pretend you can predict the future. You see that you're going to be caught off guard tomorrow by your manager coming to you with an issue with your work performance. You have an idea of what the issues may be.

1. Which "BONUS What If?" scenario listed in this chapter will you use?
2. What are some things that come to mind as you play out this situation in your head? What will be said? Think of where and at what time of day this may happen.
3. Shift to your personal life and repeat #1 and #2 above for that situation. (*See! You're becoming an expert at this already.*)

PERSONAL DEVELOPMENT CHALLENGE

Try implementing the Powerful Pause in your everyday life. Pause after others finish talking and before you respond to show them you were really listening. When you're not sure how to respond, pause again and compose your thoughts. I want to hear how you have used the Powerful Pause in your life. Contact me: **conquerstickysituations.com**

7

TYING IT ALL TOGETHER

Now for the section you've been waiting for! Examples. And lots of 'em! These examples tie the five steps together with the three-prong simple, straightforward, and human-centered approach in a nice little package so you can see how it all fits together.

Let's tie it all together! I'll start with examples of how the method applies at work, and then move on to examples we may encounter in our personal lives. Since it's not possible to detail the complete dialogue for every scenario from both sides and factor in all "What if?" scenarios, I will briefly describe what's going on in the scenario, and then focus on only what the person instigating the Sticky Conversation would say. I include relevant tips and notes in parentheses and/or italics.

I'll start with 10 example scripts relating to the workplace, from all points of views: manager, business owner, or employee. Following these work examples, I'll list 10 more examples that are non-workplace centered, and things which come up in personal life.

One piece of advice for addressing Sticky Situations that applies at work and in your personal life is not to have the conversations when you're short on time or if you're in a public space where others may overhear. Be respectful of the person you're having the conversation with. If they try to change the subject because they want to avoid conflict, gently bring them back to the topic at hand, take a deep breath, and dive into what needs to be said.

IT'S BUSINESS, BUT IT SURE FEELS PERSONAL

EXAMPLES: CONQUERING STICKY SITUATIONS AT WORK

STICKY SITUATION: The CEO's wife is in a managerial position. She's unfriendly and short with her co-workers. Many find this very upsetting because they feel like they cannot do anything about it because she's married to the CEO. (This company doesn't have a nepotism policy and gravely needs one.) Her immediate manager has been approached and asked to do something about the situation. Below shows a way he can approach this.

HOW TO HANDLE: Thanks for meeting with me today. I know you're busy. How's everything going? (Pause to see what she says. Sometimes you can learn very important things when you ask this type of question.) Your co-workers have brought a concern to my attention, and I'd like your thoughts on it. There are employees you work with who've shared that your tone comes across as irritated when they ask for updates on projects. They said you frequently respond in annoyance with, "I'll get to it, eventually!" or "Not right now!" There are two sides to every story, so I want to hear your ideas or suggestions about how to improve these interactions. What can I do to support you during the busy times so everyone can get what they need and the project can keep moving forward? (Pause—respond as appropriate.) Whether you believe what they say is accurate or not, I'll ask you to keep this perception of how you respond in mind when you interact with other employees.

> *I'll briefly address the topic of perception here. Sometimes there's a perception that someone is acting a certain way. It doesn't matter if it's true or not; the perception lives and breathes! With perceptions comes a hint of truth—similar to what they say about sarcasm. Phrasing it this way helps employees understand, whether or not they agree with it, that they may demonstrate a certain undesirable behavior. It's important that the message is clear that they need to act upon the perception and focus on improving what is within their power to control.*

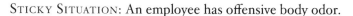

STICKY SITUATION: An employee has offensive body odor.

HOW TO HANDLE: Thank you for taking the time out of your day to meet with me. How's everything going? (Pause and listen.) I'm meeting with you today because this company values you and the work you do for us. I need to bring something up that's difficult for me to say and something that will probably be hard for you to hear. (Pause briefly again.) Your body odor is affecting others in the workplace. Our handbook policy on grooming and hygiene states as follows. (Show policy, if available. If no policy exists, omit this sentence and proceed with telling them the effect the odor has on the team.) Unwashed clothing, a need for a change in deodorant, and sometimes an underlying hygiene issue can be the cause for body odor. Has anyone brought this to your attention before? (Depending on what they say here, proceed as appropriate using the five steps to outline exactly what needs to change. You want to be crystal clear that their options are to either a) offer their own suggestions on how to improve; or b) try your suggestions. Document what is discussed so you can show (or not show) improvement when you follow up.

With body odor, other hygiene, or dress code situations, it is always good to end the conversation restating this is a hard conversation and you appreciate them being receptive and taking actions to correct the issue.

You may insert phrases in this conversation such as:

- It's important you take steps to resolve the issue because we work in tight quarters and deal with customers.
- May I share some suggestions of ways to improve this?
- I'd be happy to offer you time away from work to allow you to speak with your healthcare provider, would that be helpful?

Hygiene issues can result from many factors such as medical and mental health conditions (for example, depression can cause poor hygiene), cultural norms, problems in one's personal life, or substandard personal grooming habits. **Employers should never assume the cause of poor hygiene nor tell the employee how to improve the issue. The idea here is to offer suggestions and options for consideration.** *They should be especially careful not to violate nondiscrimination or other laws when addressing hygiene issues and requiring specific improvement. Here comes the HR nerd in me, but stay with me, this is important. Hygiene situations may trigger an interactive process to determine whether the Americans with Disabilities Act (ADA) applies. There may be an accommodation to consider to help resolve the problem. If the employee brings up a cultural or religious belief as the reason for the issue, be sure to listen first. You can tell them you'll get back to them soon to determine whether the issue still conflicts with your company's work environment and dress code and grooming standards. You may find you'll need to work with the employee to determine effective reasonable accommodation based on what they bring up. It's always best to consult with an HR or legal* *professional regarding hygiene issues if you're unsure how to handle them. Expedition HR can expertly guide you through Sticky Situations such as body odor. Visit our website to schedule a free consult at expeditionhr.com*

~

STICKY SITUATION: You're the manager of a restaurant and a server comes to you saying, "You can see through Tara's shirt, and it's making one of my tables uncomfortable."

HOW TO HANDLE: Thanks for talking with me, Tara. I know you're busy getting ready for the evening. How is everything going? (Wait and see how she responds to see if she brings up anything.) Part of my job is to ensure the best experience for our guests. I'd like to work with you to figure out a good option for this evening. Are you able to dart home and change your shirt? It is a bit too sheer. We also have some company-branded polo shirts if you wanted to try one of those. If you're ever unsure if a shirt is appropriate, I recommend bringing an alternate just in case.

Sensitivity is key with dress code. We don't want to embarrass the employee. If the employee is female and has a male manager, I recommend a female address the situation. Ideally, it will be a female in a supervisory role at the company and someone the employee knows and trusts. It's always a good idea in restaurants for there to be a back-up shirt option in case something like this comes up or someone needs a replacement shirt for another reason. If you find you're having dress code issues frequently, consider having everyone wear a uniform in your restaurant, such as standard black pants and a branded polo shirt. A nice option is to let each employee choose the style of company-provided shirt that the employee likes best. Do what makes sense for your business.

~

STICKY SITUATION: "High-Performing Jerk"—The man or woman who is highly productive, well-liked by ownership/leadership, but is a jerk and exhibits a bad attitude with those he manages and his peers. People typically avoid dealing with these issues because he's so productive and they know his work contributes heavily to the success of the company. My guess is you've interacted with someone like this in the workplace.

HOW TO HANDLE: Thanks for meeting with me since I know you're busy. How are you? (Pause and give them a chance to respond.) The company appreciates all your hard work. You make it look easy, but we know how much work you put in. (In response to your compliment, if they say something negative such as they pull all the weight of the team or that their co-workers are slackers, ask clarifying questions like, "Can you expand on what you mean?" or "Tell me more about specific instances when these things happened." Another great way to respond is with a simple "Mmmmhmm . . ." or "Hmmm . . ." to let them know you're listening.)

It's clear from what I know and from what you told me that you're a valuable member of the team. You produce excellent results through your hard work, and we're grateful for all you do. The concern is that those on your team don't always feel like it's a team environment. Some have built up resentment. (NOTE: I did not use "but" or "however.") I'd like your help brainstorming some solutions. Let's revisit in a few days. In preparation for that meeting, please put together some specific ideas that may help improve the morale on the team. Specifically, I'd like you to think of some things you may consider stopping or changing in order to bolster the relationships and morale on the team. I'll also brainstorm a list to review when we meet again.

(I always recommend giving others a chance to come to solutions on their own. This encourages buy-in. Try to avoid pushing them into a corner by telling them or strongly suggesting one way to go about things. Empowerment is key to building relationships. Don't address the situation until you have a list of at least a few suggestions from both of you. Then, go back and review the list together and decide what you can agree on and where to put effort. This is not always easy, but is worth the time and will get you and them started in the right direction with agreeable solutions.)

The tone here should not be attacking. Be careful not to place blame or imply that you're placing blame. Collect the facts about what's been happening, such as statements from employees who have complained, before you have this Sticky Conversation. Interview employees about what actions the High-Performing Jerk does to brew resentment with the team. Request specific information with dates. During your due diligence, check and see if the items fall into the categories of harassment, retaliation, or a hostile work environment. There may need to be more severe action taken if so. If the issues do not fall into those categories, at a minimum this situation would trigger a straightforward conversation on how he or she must change their behavior in order to avoid disciplinary action.

In situations where you're addressing something abstract such as a "bad attitude," focus on their behavior (such as eye rolling in meetings, loud sighing when others are talking, etc) and not simply telling them that he or she has a bad attitude. These behaviors should be witnessed by you (or someone else who is credible).

∽

STICKY SITUATION: You, as the employee, are asking for a raise.

HOW TO HANDLE: Thank you for meeting with me. I'd like to talk with you about me being deserving of a raise in June, before our annual increase in the month of January. I'm requesting a 5% increase, which would bring my salary to $52,000 a year. A few reasons I believe I'm deserving of a raise are because: (1) I trained two new employees over the last year; (2) I took on additional duties as a supervisor which have entailed longer hours and more direct reports; and (3) I completed additional projects over and above my regular duties, such as spearheading our Diversity & Inclusion committee efforts and serving as a mentor for 90 days for new employees. Thank you again for your consideration of this request. Would you be able to get me a response in one week? Do you have questions on anything I shared?

> *Having your solid reasoning, per step 3 of the five-step process, What, is key here. You need to be rock solid on what the reasons are for you being deserving of the raise in that amount. If you lack confidence or are unclear about your reasoning for making the request, it may fall on deaf ears and go nowhere.*

STICKY SITUATION: Denying a request for a raise as the employer.

HOW TO HANDLE: Hi (employee name), how are things going today? (Pause and wait for response.) Thank you for your inquiry about a raise and for being thoughtful about the reasons you deserve this. Your request was reviewed and was not approved. We made this determination because the number of direct reports you have is standard in your role, and your current pay is within range for your role, which is the 90th percentile for the job you perform. It took courage for you to ask for a raise. It also shows you're clear on wanting to take on more responsibilities and advance in the company. I'd like to continue conversations about next steps for your growth in the company. I'll set some time to talk in the next week. Do you have questions?

This response is only for illustrative purposes to show an example of how to decline a request when there was solid reasoning behind the decision. It goes without saying that the employee will not like the response. I recommend these conversations take place between the employee and their manager or with both HR and the employee's manager. It erodes the trust the HR representative needs to be truly effective if they are to take the place of the manager when delivering news of declination of a raise request.

∾

STICKY SITUATION: Providing feedback on poor performance, in this case, missing deadlines.

HOW TO HANDLE: Thank you for taking the time out of your busy day to meet with me. How are you? (Pause and wait for response.) I'd like to have a conversation about something which needs to improve with your performance regarding deadlines. You missed deadlines in May and June. In your position, deadlines are important because they ensure the work process doesn't get delayed and flows seamlessly through to the end. Occasionally, a deadline is missed because of extenuating circumstances. You are detail-oriented and when you hit the deadlines, your work is exemplary. I ask for you to do everything you can, including arranging back-up support when necessary, to keep missed deadlines from happening. I'm here to support and assist with ensuring that you're clear on your tasks and when they're due. Thanks in advance for being open to this feedback. You're valuable to the team. Do you have questions?

∽

STICKY SITUATION: A manager is terminating an employee after failure to improve work performance after being warned previously.

HOW TO HANDLE: Thank you for meeting with us. We're here today because we're letting you go. We've had prior discussions about your performance and, unfortunately, none (or not enough) of the things we hoped to see improve did. For example, we asked you to be careful with deadlines and, after our discussion in May, you missed two additional deadlines in June and July. You didn't reach out for support and when asked specifically if you needed anything, you said you were on track to meet the deadlines and not to worry. We made this decision because deadlines are important to the products we deliver to our customers. We appreciate the work you did for us and for all the successes you were a big part of. I'm sorry to deliver this news today. Thank you again for your work with the company.

In terminations, after delivering the key pieces above, transition to review of their parting benefits details, returning of company property, etc. Be sure to provide them with documents reviewing what you covered. Keep in mind, they may not remember what you tell them. Offering the information in written form shows that you care for them on this hard day of losing their job.

∽

STICKY SITUATION: An employee approaches you, their manager, and asks, "Am I getting fired?"

HOW TO HANDLE: Thanks for coming forward. You are on thin ice, which should not be a surprise based on recent performance conversations. So yes, there are concerns about your future with the company. We haven't made the final determination, but there are discussions happening. This is all I can share with you.

If they ask for more information, you may want to respond with, "I can only repeat what I told you." If they ask if they should be looking for a job, you can say, "That is a determination you need to make." This may or may not satisfy the employee. Be ready to repeat yourself and assert unequivocally when the conversation is over. Many say too much in these situations. They feel cornered and end up saying something they regret or sharing too much confidential information. In this situation, let's say that the employee is likely going to get fired, and you knew this as a fact when he asked the question. It is still not your place to disclose this to him just yet, so responding per the script is a good way to be straightforward, while not disclosing the final confidential details.

STICKY SITUATION: An employee asks if they're getting fired and shares that they're actively searching for a job. They want advice about whether to quit.

HOW TO HANDLE: Thank you for coming to speak with me and sharing your concerns. I can see how this would be a tough spot to be in. We haven't made the final determination about next steps with your employment. Having feelers out there for your next opportunity might not be a bad idea. If it were me, I might be doing the same.

The employee may even thank you for being straightforward! It has happened to me in my experience. Their position at the company is fragile. You would do them a disservice if you lead them to think their position is secure. I'd prefer this type of straightforward response if I were in their position. As you

learned in the straightforward section, humans dislike
uncertainty. Having information, any information, often makes
us feel better about a situation and even more empowered to
control our related actions. Therefore, being candid about an
imminent firing may give the employee a sense of peace in
knowing the reality.

The goal is to never have an employee surprised when their
employment ends. A way of ensuring this doesn't happen is being
straightforward in all communications with the employee. There
will also ideally include previous straightforward disciplinary
conversations that lead up to the termination.

THIS TIME, IT'S PERSONAL

EXAMPLES: CONQUERING STICKY SITUATIONS IN LIFE

STICKY SITUATION: You're shopping for an interview outfit with a dear girlfriend. From the dressing room, she tells you she has made her decision to purchase that outfit which she just had on and showed you. You're a bit surprised with her choice because you think it looks unprofessional. You worry if she wears it, it may cost her the interview. You quickly see you are in a Sticky Situation and know you need to say something.

HOW TO HANDLE: I love that you asked me to come along shopping with you today! I'm really excited about your promising job opportunity. I really like the outfit you chose for casual events and everyday work. If it were me, I may choose something a little dressier for the interview. I want you to have the best chance at getting this new job. I'll grab a few other options for you to try if you're up for it? (At that point, you hope your friend understands that you're nicely saying you don't like what she chose and that she lets you grab other options to try. Hopefully, from there, she chooses one that's more professional.)

∼

STICKY SITUATION: You have a good friend who surprised you by asking you out on a date. You love your friendship and really don't want that kind of relationship.

HOW TO HANDLE: I'm so flattered! I absolutely love hanging out with you. It would be unfair of me to not be honest and tell you that I'm not interested in us dating. I hope we can continue as friends because you're incredibly special to me.

∼

STICKY SITUATION: You're at a work event and a co-worker just won't leave you alone. He's incessantly talking to you about work stuff. You're bored stiff and need to escape.

HOW TO HANDLE: (Jump in when there is a lull in the conversation—you need to be fast!) It was nice chatting with you. I enjoyed hearing about [insert what the conversation was about]. I'm going to go say hi to a few others now. I hope you enjoy the rest of the party! (Then, make your escape!)

∼

STICKY SITUATION: You're venting about someone in an email and then realize you sent it to the person you were venting about. He confronts you before you're able to get to him.

HOW TO HANDLE: I'm sorry for the situation—I handled it very poorly. (Don't say you didn't mean what you wrote, because that's lying, and they won't believe you anyway. This is one of those good places for a sincere apology. You messed up, and you need to own it.) I should have been straightforward and addressed the issues directly with you in the first place. I owe it to you to have a conversation about what I wrote in the email. (See if they're receptive to that. Be honest about what the issues are and tell them you would like to work together to solve the issues. It's okay to tell them you are frustrated. Being straightforward is key here if you want resolution.) Again, I handled this poorly. I learned a lesson here that I should bring up the issues directly with the other person. I value our relationship and hope that you can forgive me. (The other person may even gain respect for you for the way you handled this and get over the actual issue itself quicker than expected.)

∾

STICKY SITUATION: You're having a conversation with a friend and suddenly, out of left field, he says something hurtful to you about how he interpreted one of your past actions.

HOW TO HANDLE: Thank you for saying something. It was never my intention to make you feel that way. (Don't deny what he called you out about unless it was an inaccurate statement, in which case, correct him with the factual truth. If what he said is true, own it. This may be another good place for a sincere apology. Even if you disagree that whatever you did was hurtful, you want to preserve the friendship, so keep that in mind.) I learned a lesson here that sometimes things can be interpreted differently by different people. I value our friendship and hope that you always feel like you can bring up things like this in the future.

∾

STICKY SITUATION: A friend is always borrowing things.

HOW TO HANDLE: Hey, I wanted to get back to you about your request to borrow our paddleboards. That won't work for this weekend. I'm hoping we can chat quick about you borrowing my things. You're a good friend, and I'm happy to lend you things on occasion. It seems your requests have been happening a lot lately. There are also certain things I prefer not to lend. Thanks for understanding.

Remember to call on being empathetic if your friend is having money struggles and that's why they're borrowing things. At the same time, don't let this stop you from saying what you need to say if you have reasons for feeling this way.

Not being clear on boundaries can sometimes lead to passive aggressive behavior. It's important to be firm about what you will and won't allow. Don't let those lines get blurry or you'll end up feeling frustrated. Boundaries with borrowing looks like setting parameters on when and how much someone can borrow. Other times, it may be not allowing any borrowing. Set boundaries that you are comfortable with—and be 100% okay with them! It is easier to say no when you have boundaries set. If you know of an option where your friend can either rent or buy the item they're always borrowing from you, recommend it. Also, if you're thinking of selling what they keep borrowing, let them know. Be upfront if you're willing to sell it to them and for what price.

The best thing about boundaries is that once you set them regularly, those around you will get the hint. If they're not receptive or respectful of your boundaries on lending your things, maybe they're not deserving of your friendship. One-sided friendships can drain you. (See chapter 8, "Know When to Hold 'Em and Know When to Fold 'Em.")

∼

STICKY SITUATION: You offered to help an elderly neighbor with her grocery shopping when the pandemic began. You've done it for about three months, and it's starting to take too much time.

You need to tell her you can no longer do it. She is a dear friend and you care about her and her health.

HOW TO HANDLE: Thanks for taking a minute to chat with me. How are you? (Pause and see what she says.) Starting next week, I can no longer shop for your groceries. I care about your well-being and don't want you to feel stressed during COVID. I want to help ensure you have the resources you need, so I've put together a list of grocery delivery services and options for you to do curbside pickup at the grocery stores in town. I'm happy to answer questions now, or feel free to let me know if questions arise in the future. Thanks again for understanding that I can no longer do this for you.

STICKY SITUATION: Requesting a refund for poor service.

HOW TO HANDLE: Thanks for your time to speak with me. How are you today? (Pause and listen to their response. This acknowledges that there is another human on the other end of the line or in front of you, depending on how you are addressing the issue. This is a business transaction and not personal towards them. You are upset about the service you received, but want to remember to keep that separate from the way you address the rep with whom you speak with to request the refund.) I'm contacting you because I'd like a refund in the amount of $500 for the online subscription. I'd like a refund because the service is not to the standard I was promised upon signing up. I never received the promised materials, and my service did not start for seven weeks after I signed up. I'll look for this refund in the next week. Do you need anything else from me to get this processed? Thank you for expediting my refund.

Go into the conversation knowing the outcome you expect. Your words should align with your firm expectation.

~

STICKY SITUATION: You are criticized for your new business venture by a family member and want to address it.

HOW TO HANDLE: Hey, I value our relationship and don't want this to create awkwardness, which is why I need to bring it up. Though you may not have intended to, when you say [insert what the criticism is here], it hurts my feelings. I've been working hard to build this business. It's something I'm very proud of. I find the words you've used to be hurtful. I'd be happy to answer questions about my business if you want to know more. Even if you don't have an interest in what I'm doing, I ask that you do not say these things to me or say them when we're around others. Thank you for listening.

~

STICKY SITUATION: Your daycare provider is always giving your kids unhealthy snacks.

HOW TO HANDLE: Thanks for taking the time to chat with me. How are things going? (Pause and give them a chance to respond.) My kids have such a good time here, and I know they're well taken care of. Not all daycares are the same, and I'm grateful they come here. My kids have told me about the snacks they receive. Are there options for healthier snacks? If not, I'm happy to send along some for them. I wanted to check on other options before I do. (Pause to let them reply.) Thanks again for taking a minute to chat with me and for being open to these other options. I appreciate all the work you all do to care for the kids.

I hope these examples were helpful. For even more examples, visit: **conquerstickysituations.com/moreexamples**

RECAP

So, you've decided your issue needs addressing. You've learned about the simple five-step, three-prong approach. You've read a whole, whole bunch of examples. Now, it's time to take what you learned, take a deep breath, and have the Sticky Conversation. You got this!

YOU GOT THIS! LET'S TIE IT ALL TOGETHER AND ACTUALLY WRITE A PRACTICE SCRIPT . . .

Here is a quick reminder of 5-step process:

1. Thanks
2. Why
3. What
4. How
5. Thanks Again

Take what you put together in previous You Got This! exercises and fill in the spaces below.

Your Sticky Situation details:

_____

_____

_____

How to handle/What you will say:

_____

_____

_____

_____

PERSONAL DEVELOPMENT CHALLENGE

All too often, we breeze right by our wins and don't even notice when we grow and stretch ourselves. You just wrote a sample script, which means you're already on your way to conquering your Sticky Situation! Take a minute to reflect on that win and where you have come since you started reading this book—sit in the sun, take a nap, or maybe treat yourself to your favorite snack. Do something to celebrate!

8

KNOW WHEN TO HOLD 'EM, KNOW WHEN TO FOLD 'EM

I'm not here to tell you that after you have the Sticky Conversation, everything will be unicorns and rainbows from there on out. After you say your piece, you and the other person may not see eye-to-eye. They may outright disagree and tell you what you said is wrong or unfounded. My goal in providing the "What If?" chapter was to share scenarios like this, which may happen as you go about navigating Sticky Situations. I also gave you tools for when Sticky Conversations catch you off guard. While I hope the "What If?" chapter helped you, it would be unrealistic for either of us to think this book will solve every problem and always get you to the resolution you want or need. The goal of the book is to set you up to broach the tough conversation initially—through the five steps.

As Kenny Rogers says in his song, "The Gambler," "You've got to know when to hold 'em/know when to fold 'em/know when to walk away/and know when to run." If you address a Sticky Situation and find yourself met with huge resistance, I can't tell you how far to push, or if pushing back makes sense. There are so many types of situations and no one-size-fits-all approach. There's no crystal ball that can tell you when to push back and when to walk away. Where to go after the initial conversation is something you need to assess. Don't go it alone. Reach out to a trusted friend or co-worker to ask their advice. See what they recommend. Talk to a therapist or seek a coach who can help you make this determination of how to proceed with your personal goals. They may help you sift through what's going on and get clear on whether it's worth your energy to go up against the resistance. They may help you figure out if you should fold 'em and walk away.

In my interactions with employees who came to me asking if they were going to get fired, I felt it lacked integrity if I were to paint a rosy picture for them that everything was fine or that big problems were minor. I often used this exact "Know when to hold 'em and know when to fold 'em" expression in these conversations. I told them they have control over certain things and not others, and they needed to choose how far they wanted to go with trying to fix the issues. Part of that was assessing whether fixing those issues was even under their control or something they wanted to put effort toward. There comes a point where we need to weigh whether it's worth pushing against the barrier(s) or if it is time to walk away.

To be clear, when we walk away from something in life, it doesn't mean we're failing or weak. In fact, it's a sign of strength to recognize when a situation is hopeless. How much we'll take before we say, "No more!" is a direct reflection of our boundaries.

Successful people have this skill mastered. They know when to dig in their heels, push back against resistance, and persevere until they come out the other side. But, they're also successful because they know when to cut their losses and move on. Life is short. Don't let yourself be emotionally beat up before you decide enough is enough and walk away. Think of Kenny when you come up against a barrier and are unsure if you should push or not. Be good to yourself—you only have this one life.

PERSONAL DEVELOPMENT CHALLENGE

To see if you should hold 'em or fold 'em, try this exercise to look within and assess whether you're being true to yourself if you decide not to address the issue. For the pros, list the ways that addressing the conversation could improve your relationship or work situation. For the cons, list the ways it could hurt the relationship or make the situation at work worse. Sometimes, the choice to fold 'em means that you move on from the relationship or work situation instead of addressing the issue. Writing out the pros and cons will force you consider all possible outcomes and allow you to make the best judgement. It's okay to be unsure if what you decide is the best choice. This exercise is not always easy, but doing it will help you make the best decision with the information available to you at this present moment. Take a minute to sit quietly before doing this Personal Development Challenge and breathe. You got this! I have outlined this all below for you to fill in.

HOLD 'EM/HAVE THE CONVERSATION | ProsCons

1.

2.

3.

FOLD 'EM/NOT HAVE THE CONVERSATION | ProsCons

1.

2.

3.

9

GET THE WIGGLES OUT

My puppy, Sprout, was four months old when we adopted him. If you have ever had a puppy, you know they wiggle in excitement at, well, everything. When we give puppies opportunities to work out their boundless energy, I call it, "getting their wiggles out"—whether it be through exercise, discipline, or training. They're like little fully charged batteries at the start of each day. Working out these wiggles is essential. You'll have greater chances of raising a terrific dog if you devote time to getting their wiggles out first thing each day. If you don't, your sweet puppy will drive you bonkers and likely chew up your couch.

I believe we have some form of wiggles we need to get out each day, too. If you're like me, your mind races nonstop and you need to work out your own wiggles before you can function at your best. This is why I call this my "Get the WIGGLES Out" morning routine, or the "WIGGLES" routine for short. This is my secret weapon and I'll share all the details with you here. This routine will get you focused and prepared to deal with any Sticky Situation that comes your way.

Before we go any further, let's discuss what each letter in the WIGGLES morning routine acronym stands for:

- W—Wear and Water (evening before)
- I—Intentions (evening before)
- G—Gratitude
- G—Growth
- L—Loosen and Listen
- E—Examination of Self
- S—Send it!

This routine isn't rigid. In fact, the order of the WIGGLES routine doesn't really matter as long as you make sure not to skip the Intentions step.

You can spend as much time as you'd like on each step, but I recommend allowing at least 20 minutes to experience the positive effects of this routine in your life. You also don't need to do all the steps every morning. Play with it, and do what feels best for you.

You may notice that exercise isn't part of the actual WIGGLES routine. Setting the intention for how you'll exercise *is*. If you want to jump-start your day with exercise first, do it! Exercise is a great way to get the blood pumping. I enjoy sitting with my coffee and going through my WIGGLES routine before I exercise. It inspires me to feel like I've already accomplished something when I head into my workout.

Steps W & I: The Evening Before (5-10 minutes)

W—WEAR AND WATER

Wear: Does this bring you back to your mom telling you to set out your clothes for school the next day? (My mom did!) If you ever set your clothes out as an adult, you know how it eliminates a decision in the morning and can help add to a sense of control and calm to your day, first thing. You only have so much energy to make decisions in a day. This step helps you eliminate one decision and save your remaining "decision bank" for more important things throughout the day. Let's say you have about 15 decisions in your "tank" each day before you feel depleted. If you use one of them first thing in the morning deciding what to wear, you're already 6% through your daily decision allotment. What a waste! Lay out your workout/comfy/work clothes the night before in a place where you can turn on a light and get dressed and not disturb others. Ensure you have everything down to your socks and undies ready to get dressed quickly and effortlessly.

Want proof this works? Steve Jobs and Albert Einstein are examples of two people who understood protecting decisions. They wore the same or similar outfit every day. They knew they were wasting brainpower to pick out a new outfit each morning. Plan your outfit the night before and save your mental decision power.

Water: When you sleep, your body gets dehydrated. For this reason, I suggest putting some water in a place where you can easily access it when you wake up. Here's a list of what chugging down some water first thing in the morning does for you:

- Cleanses your bowels
- Flushes toxins from the body
- Prevents headaches
- Increases energy
- Speeds up your metabolism (helps with weight loss)
- Improves your skin
- Promotes healthy hair
- Prevents kidney stones
- Strengthens immune system

Did I convince you? If not, try it for a day or two and see how you feel. From there, you can decide if it's right for you. There are no rules here—only suggestions. Do what's best for you.

I–INTENTIONS

There are three types of intentions I'd like for you to set in this part of the WIGGLES routine:

1. Exercise
2. Growth
3. Action items

EXERCISE

Note which type of exercise you will do that day. The important thing here is to schedule daily exercise, no matter how short, into your calendar, so you're sure it happens. Having a healthy physical body promotes a healthy mind, and a healthy mind is a productive mind.

GROWTH

This is where you will simply determine what you will do during the growth part of the routine and set needed materials aside, like books, magazines, or maybe downloading a Podcast. The key is to have these things ready so as not to waste the precious morning time preparing.

ACTION ITEMS

List one to three action items that you want to accomplish during your morning routine. I don't recommend more than three action items because, as Jim Collins, author of the book, *Good to Great*, says, "If you have more than three priorities, you have none." Don't take on more than is realistic for the time frame you allot for your morning routine. When making this list, estimate the time needed to complete each task. This will help in determining how many action items you should plan on accomplishing. This estimation of time for key action items will be a work in progress. A tip I can give you is to overestimate how long things will take so that you feel satisfied at the end of your morning routine. Review the time you allotted for each so you mentally prepare for what you're going to work on. To make your list of action items, try thinking of action items which will:

- Propel you personally or your business forward in some impactful way
- Require a high level of focus (mornings can be magic for productivity if you are a morning person)
- Need to be done today or this week

Specific action items which fall under the above categories may be:

- Sending one important email
- Brainstorming action steps for a new and exciting project
- Mapping out the week's meal plan
- Working on your resume
- Writing a chapter of a book
- Outlining next steps for your side hustle business

G–GRATITUDE

Write three things for which you're grateful. That's it! Gratitude has a snowball effect. Once you practice gratitude, you become more aware of it. Before you know it, you'll start thinking grateful thoughts during the day without even intending to.

The things you're grateful for don't need to be big. Don't overthink this. Just write whatever comes to mind. And, by all means, don't quit at three if you have more!

While gratitude is a very important step, it's also very flexible. There is no one right way to practice gratitude. The important thing is to incorporate it somehow into every morning to see its amazing and compounding effects.

G-GROWTH

This is where you call upon the materials you set aside in the Intentions step. You may want to listen to a podcast or choose to read a few pages of a book or an article on a topic about which you want to learn and grow your knowledge. When I say grow your knowledge, it doesn't need to be in your career area. It could be in any area where you want to learn more, such as how to knit, how to flip houses, or maybe how to better manage your finances. One of my favorite books to read during my growth time is *The Daily Stoic*, by Ryan Holiday and Stephen Hanselman. This is a fantastic thought-provoking read broken out into short snippets for each day of the year.

There's so much to do every day that we can easily forget we need to keep growing and learning or else we risk becoming stagnant and bored. Whatever you choose for your growth time —enjoy it! This is one of my favorite parts of the morning since personal growth is a core value of mine.

In your professional life, you become more of an asset to your workplace the more you stay current on relevant topics to your field. If you're looking to change careers, this learning will help you transition faster. There are so many amazing ways to use this growth time to grow yourself personally and professionally.

L-LOOSEN & LISTEN

Loosen: In this step, I want you to actually wiggle your body and shake off anything negative weighing on you, similarly to if you were gently shaking the water off of your hands. Visualize any negativity or stress from yesterday literally falling off you. You may only need to do it for a few seconds or maybe longer will feel good. Add or replace this loosening exercise with stretches if you prefer.

Listen: Sit quietly and listen, not to physical sounds but to whatever needs to come to you from the universe. I believe the universe sends us messages constantly. Some call it instinct or your "gut." I call these messages shoulder "taps" from the universe because they're nearly unrecognizable. They also come at some of the most random times. If you are not into this, feel free to jump to the next section. If you like this idea of getting in tune with the universe, I invite you to do a related exercise. Over the next week, try to listen and be aware of the taps. By listening, I mean nothing more than being aware of when things "pop into your head." Don't overcomplicate it.

Note when you receive a tap and what the message is. Be aware because the taps can come at the most random times such as when you are in the shower, walking the dog, or sitting at work. Don't judge the messages or try to analyze right then; just note them. If you aren't sure if something was a tap, note it anyway. (It probably is a tap.)

At the end of the week, if you noted many taps, great! This means you're tuning in and the universe is talking to you. If not, no problem. If you want to keep at it, try listening for a few more days. Be aware, some taps will repeat. I'll talk more about this in a minute.

If you experienced numerous taps, you're likely ready for the next step. Did you note any repeat taps? If you hear a tap once, it's not necessarily insignificant, but isn't something I believe you need to pay much attention. Watch for two of the same taps . . . this *could* mean something significant. If you hear three taps, this is a definite call to look closer at the messages. By looking closer, I mean to think a little more deeply about what these taps, or messages, could mean. Taps are amazing and powerful but aren't always totally clear. Sometimes, three taps come in the form of:

- Not being able to get your mind off something
- Having a "nagging" feeling about something
- Everything you do throughout the day makes you think of this one thing

If you enjoy meditating or would like to try it during this part of your morning, there are many wonderful free online resources available. You can easily locate short meditations by searching online for "Five-minute meditation" (or 10 or 20 minutes depending on how long you want to meditate). I especially like the short (five minutes or less) meditations by The Honest Guys. When you find something good to listen to, breathe and focus on the meditation. As you take the breaths, focus on long exhales, pushing all the air out and waiting a second or two before you inhale again. This quiet and/or meditation time and deep breathing calms our bodies and minds enabling us to think clearly and come up with solutions, solutions that can easily get lost in the busyness of life when we're moving too fast.

This step will train your mind to be still, which will then hone your skills with listening to the taps. I listened to these taps and they truly changed my life. I was prompted to start my business and write this book from taps. I believe they have the potential to change your life too. What if you turned and looked at what these taps are trying to tell you?

If this section about the taps resonated with you, check out *You are a Badass*, by Jen Sincero. She goes much deeper with the idea of tapping into the universe and manifesting good things. I think all her books are phenomenal. Her audiobooks are an added treat.

In life, we often put things off without even realizing we are doing so. If you get three taps about a Sticky Situation in your life, look closer at it. It may be trying to tell you, "Conquer this Sticky Situation!"

E-EXAMINATION OF SELF

Quiet time from the last step gives your mind a chance to be still and fosters looking inward. Some questions you can reflect on during this time may be:

- In which areas of my life do I feel I need the most growth?
- Which areas do I feel I've made strides to improve?

Try writing three things you want to bring more of into your life, such as being present with your partner or kids or maybe finding more balance in your life. Notice I'm not asking you what you want less of in your life. The intent here is to not focus on things you want to do less of. Focus on the things you want more of because you have more control over those things.

You can add to the list each day or start anew each day. Either way, keep the list so you can look back and see what you listed previously. It's interesting to see how they change over time.

S-SEND IT!

This one needed an exclamation point—because it should feel super satisfying!

This last letter of the acronym comes from a funny scene that happened one summer night as my family enjoyed dinner with friends outside in our backyard. There were three teenagers in the yard behind ours who had climbed on top of their garden shed. We quickly became interested in what they were doing. Suddenly, one leapt from the top of the shed yelling, "Send it!" He landed with a huge bounce on the trampoline, followed by huge fits of laughter and hoots from his buddies urging the next kid to do the same. The others followed suit also shouting "Send it!" every time they leapt from the shed and landed with a huge bounce on the trampoline. We found this scene incredibly entertaining and funny. I found it only fitting to call this last step of the WIGGLES routine "Send it!" because this is the step where you get pumped about the next "leap" for your business or for your personal life, that action item that will push you forward.

To determine which item to start with, refer back to what you prepared from the Intentions step.

Now you know how to "Get the Wiggles Out" and implement a solid morning routine. This will center you for your day and give you the space to practice and reflect on what you learned. A morning routine has truly transformed my days, and I hope it can do the same for you. Tell me about how it goes! Contact me: **conquerstickysituations.com**

YOU GOT THIS!

A purple ribbon is safety clipped to my biking backpack in memory of Cyndi. Each time I prepare to ride and see the ribbon, I think of Cyndi and the glorious memories of riding together, but also of what an inspiration she was to me. I learned how to be a better biker, but I also learned to better navigate my life when things get technical or "sticky." I say to myself, "C'mon Jill . . . keep on pedaling and don't freak out. You'll get through this and anything else that comes your way." If Cyndi only knew the impact she had on me with these words!

You can no longer use the excuse that no one exposed you to techniques on how to handle Sticky Situations. Now you have, and it's time to act. Conquering a difficult situation can be scary, and downright hard! You can do it—I know you can. It will get easier if you commit to using the five-step formula and applying the simple, straightforward, and human-centered approach. I know it works because I've seen it work time and time again with those I've shared it with in my personal life, in past workplaces, and with my consulting clients.

I can't promise you this will always be easy. I *can* promise that if you keep at it, it will get easier. There will be stressful moments, and one thing you can be sure of is that there will always be Sticky Situations to deal with. That's life. Take a deep breath. Use the WIGGLES routine to get centered for your day and to prepare yourself for when it's time to conquer the Sticky Situation. Be easy on yourself as you grow your skills to become better. And, as my daughter Jenna reminded us, it never hurts to have donuts handy when having Sticky Conversations.

I (hopefully) kept you entertained with stories and anecdotes from my work and life experiences, and have given you practical and helpful exercises to implement what you learned. Now that you've finished this book, you may be excited or perhaps nervous about implementing what you learned. Don't let the "What if?" scenarios paralyze you into inaction. Rather, plan how you'll approach your next Sticky Situation. I hope you can also use and get value from my WIGGLES morning routine.

Please Promise

Please promise me you'll keep going when the going gets tough. Don't avoid difficult situations because you're afraid of the outcome. It's okay if someone else doesn't see eye-to-eye with your point of view.

You can conquer the awkwardness and fear of confronting life's stickiest moments if you just keep your feet firmly planted on the pedals—pushing them around and around until eventually you're making your way through obstacles you once thought were impassable. Don't wait, the time is now!

I'd Love Your Help

Please share this book! I need your help spreading the word to help one more person conquer a Sticky Situation that's been causing them headaches, heartache, or an even worse type of stress or pain. Gift it to someone who needs it. Or even better, offer to read it and together help each other handle a Sticky Situation one or both of you have been dreading.

Suggest this book for your next book club. You never know who it will resonate deeply with who then will feel empowered with new hope to overcome a situation they once thought was insurmountable. You have a great opportunity to change another life through sharing this book.

If you're a manager or business owner, consider purchasing copies of this book for your team. Empower your biggest asset, your employees, with the right tools to handle their own Sticky Situations at work and in their personal lives. Incorporate it into your trainings. Contact Expedition HR for an on-site training or visit **conquerstickysituations.com** for other resources.

If my approach to Sticky Situations resonated with you and you want to receive more great tips, visit **expeditionhr.com** and sign up for our newsletter.

I thank you sincerely for spreading this important message with the world around you.

RESOURCES

Find links to these books and additional resources at **conquerstickysituations.com**:

- *The Daily Stoic*, by Ryan Holiday and Stephen Hanselman
- *The Life Changing Magic of Tidying Up*, by Marie Kondo
- *Atomic Habits*, by James Clear
- *Good to Great*, by Jim Collins
- *You are a Badass Every Day*, by Jen Sincero

ACKNOWLEDGMENTS

To my husband Dan and kids: Thank you for your endless support and encouragement on this book writing journey. I'm so grateful to you three incredible beings.

To my parents, Bob and Mary (aka "Gram" and "Pep"), for always being my biggest fans.

To Henry Weeks, for giving me one of my most formative HR job experiences.

To my editors, Sky Nuttal and Kim Ledgerwood, for giving me straightforward feedback.

To my proofreader Devon Tuggle, for being so patient with me and my endless questions.

To my awesome beta-readers: Suzanne St. Pierre, Hilary Lyon and Cindy Lanza - love you ladies.

To the entire team at Cutting Edge Studios – Joris, Danijela, and Michael. Thanks for your guidance and encouragement to get me to the finish line.

ABOUT THE AUTHOR

Jill lives in the mountains of Park City, Utah, with her husband, two kids, puppy, and 16-year-old "Queen of the House" cat. A self-proclaimed HR nerd, Jill loves to travel, bike, speak Spanish, and ski deep powder. Jill is the founder and CEO of Expedition HR Consulting—and a professional Sticky Situation solver.

Expedition HR helps small, start-up, and growing businesses quickly learn exactly what they need to know about HR to mitigate risk. Expedition HR simply and straightforwardly guides its clients in knowing how to hire and retain the right people, how to let people go with compassion, and how to navigate the stickiest employee situations. Expedition HR proudly donates a portion of each dollar earned. With over two decades of human resources experience and a Professional in Human Resources (PHR) certification, Jill's vast experience renders her an expert in her field.

To learn more about working with Expedition HR, or to join the Expedition HR newsletter to receive tips and tricks about Sticky Situations, visit **expeditionhr.com**.

EXPEDITION **HR**

CAN YOU HELP?

Sharing my message through buying this book for someone who needs it would mean the world to me!

Please leave me an honest review on Amazon letting me know what you thought of the book.
I need your input to make future books the best they can be.

Thank you again for reading!

I am grateful for you,
Jill Shroyer

NOTES

NOTES

NOTES

NOTES

NOTES

Made in the USA
Columbia, SC
17 October 2021